TALES FROM THE
GRID SQUARE

STORIES OF PARANORMAL
MILITARY EXPERIENCES

VOLUME I

By Nick Orton

Front Cover Artist Credit

A special thank you to Herb Ascherman for the incredible artwork featured on the cover. He is an amazing artist, as well as a fellow enthusiast of the paranormal!

Please check out and support his excellent artwork on his Instagram account: @swreck972.

Acknowledgments

A special thank you to the following individuals for their mentorship and friendship:

Wes Gramer (Sasquatch Chronicles Podcast)

Tony Merkal (The Confessionals Podcast)

SGT Nicholas Laidlaw, USMC (Battles and Beers, @battles.and.beers)

Kyle Ross, aka "Discord Kyle"

Amanda Marie (IG: @saltykilo)

"Not a JTAC" (IG: @not.a.jtac_);

Staff Morale Page (IG: @staff_morale_page_)

My family and friends who helped indulge my interest in all of this!

Disclaimer

The contents of this book **_ARE NOT_** reflective of the Department of Defense and Armed Services.

The contents of this book **_DO NOT_** serve as any sort of official statement by the Department of Defense and Armed forces.

The views expressed in this book are of a personal nature and **NOT RELATED** to any official view of the Department of Defense and the Armed Services.

Minimal editing has taken place to present these stories to the reader to preserve the voice of the original source. As a discretion, the stories printed are presented in their **RAW AND VULGAR FORM**. This book contains depictions of violence and language that can be disturbing to some.

As you read these stories, please remember: **IT IS 100% IMPOSSIBLE FOR ME TO VERIFY THESE STORIES**, so take these stories with a "grain of salt." These stories are presented to you on the good faith that the source is telling the truth.

TABLE OF CONTENTS

FORWARD

There is an unspoken stigma within the Armed Forces of talking about events that are not "normal." Lets just say you begin to hear voices in your house, the first question they ask you at Behavioral Health is: "Are your hearing voices?" This isn't an attack on the military Behavioral Health system, but to my point… what if you are mentally sound? What if the voices you are hearing aren't in your head? What if there's something else going on entirely? Who can you talk to without fear of being stigmatized? So you just keep your lips sealed and drive on. But all the while, you are left shaken by experiences you cannot explain.

During "The Lockdown" of 2020, I came across an Instagram Story where military members shared their experiences with the "paranormal." I was blown away (and a little spooked myself) at what I was reading. But I started to wonder: how many more people had stories they were holding onto?

Like most great ideas, "Tales From The Grid Square" was created after a couple of drinks. I have always been interested in the paranormal, one of those hobbies that will have you going down rabbit holes researching mysteries, cryptids, and UFOs. After having some experiences of my own (both in and out of the service) and hearing stories from others, I decided that I wanted to enhance Service Member's and veteran voices in my own unique way. So I created an Instagram page and got to work.

Being a Service Member myself, I aimed for "Tales From the Grid Square" to be a resource that allows Service Members and Veterans a way to share their stories anonymously. Anonymity is the vital ingredient to "Tales From The Grid Square". The stories are always anonymous (unless otherwise specified). This is a Veteran run operation as well (a one man show I might add), allowing Veterans to share unique stories without fear of reprisal or ridicule.

You are about to read **240** accounts from Active-Duty Service Members, National Guardsmen, Reservists, Veterans, and their families. These stories have been selected because they best demonstrate both the military experience combined with a paranormal one. The words you will read are the raw, unfiltered and true words of those that have experienced things from the mundane to events that defy normality.

Many of these stories come directly from the Instagram page, email, and first-hand accounts in the many threads of Reddit and Internet blogs. I have spent countless man hours in the many nooks and crannies of the internet looking for these stories and offering myself as a resource to those with a story to tell.

These stories are not intended to provide one hundred percent irrefutable proof of the paranormal. I did not write this book to convince you to believe or not to believe. Instead, I share these stories with you to give a voice to Veterans and Service Members who have had experiences that defy normality.

If you enjoy these stories and want to explore the topic of "Military Paranormal," please check out the Instagram page and spread the word. The bigger the net, the bigger the catch. There are some truly incredible stories out there, and I need your help to find the truly incredible people who can tell them. Feel free to share and reach out to me! Thank you so much for your support!

Very Respectfully,

Nick
Founder of Tales From The Grid Square
Instagram: @Tales_From_The_Gridsquare
Email: Talesfromthegridsquare@gmail.com

"Nothing beats the terror that we pass off at the moment…"

- Anonymous US Army Soldier

UNITED STATES ARMY

AT WAR

The Invisible Man

My second deployment to Iraq. We were doing a nighttime Small Kill Team (SKT) ambush in a house we took over while overwatching an intersection commonly planted with Improvised Explosive Device (IED), trying to kill the idiots who emplace them.

Dawn was coming up. We were just ready to pack up and call the Quick Reaction Force (QRF) platoon to drive up and pick us up when we spotted a lone dude carrying an artillery round. It was too bright for any night vision, still a bit dark for eyes, but we positively ID'd as a hostile threat, and I had my sniper with an M110 kill him.

One-shot, only about 175 meters, easy shot. Upper chest, I was on glass and saw bullet impact. I watched him crumple and drop in the grass on the side of the road. He was a skinny fucker wearing a tight athletic shirt. He didn't have body armor to stop 7.62 NATO at that range.

I called QRF to pick us up and reported to the command. Command orders us to search the kill. As they were driving up, my SKT team (an infantry fireteam plus a sniper team) left the house to check the body for intel, because we had to bag them and drop them off at the local Iraqi police station if possible. But there was no body. WHAT THE FUCK?

We walked around for like 20 minutes, ever-enlarging circles. Not a fucking single piece of evidence he was there. No body, no blood, no crawl marks, no IED, no nothing. We looked like idiots because I'd reported the shot on the company network and no body. Caught an endless amount of shit about it. But weird shit happens in war. A few years later, I ran into a dude who served in the unit we relieved in place. They left; we took over the area of operations. We were at a bar, putting drinks away and trading war stories about the neighborhoods and shit. Then I brought up that area we dropped the "invisible man" (what I came to call him). I didn't tell the story. I just mentioned the frequency of IEDs at that intersection area.

Then he tells a story. About an SKT who killed an IED emplacer but didn't find the body. No fucking way! Now he wasn't there, but it was another platoon in his company whose squad was out and reported they'd smoked the guy. So he knew part of their story. He didn't have a description of appearance. But in his version, many dudes had opened on the emplacer, a few M4s, a M249, and a M240, and they were so sure they got him. No way someone survived that barrage. They dumped nearly a hundred rounds at one dude.

What are the chances of two dudes with lousy luck who have been mortally wounded in the same place a year apart? Shot but not killed instantly. Shock hits them, no pain. Clothes absorbed the blood. The low crawl away to some dead space we can't see, where they get up, make it a few blocks before dying—just a coincidence. No evidence was found, no IED, etc. That has to be it.

Otherwise, was it a ghost? Did we all hallucinate? Sometimes I can't sleep because of the Invisible Man. If that was a ghost, then there is an afterlife. What happens to me when I go? Will the Invisible Man be waiting for me?

Mosul

My mom deployed to Iraq with the Army, to Mosul, and told me (I don't remember if it was her experience or someone else's experience, but we'll say it was hers for now) in 2006. She was manning a traffic control point (TCP) as part of the "Lioness Team" (female engagement team's predecessor) with some grunts.

The TCP was set on a road leading to a mosque/church. One night, a car pulls up, and the driver looks scared and nervous, and in the passenger seat was a woman in hijab-wearing sunglasses or some shit.

Anyway, the Soldier asks the guy who's in the driver's seat for IDs and my mom to go to the passenger seat and deal with the passenger. My mom walks over to order the woman to pull down her hijab from her face and take her glasses off, or whatever was concealing her face.

The woman doesn't move at all, so my mom and the other guy order the driver to remove her face coverings, and the dude starts nervously trembling and removes her face coverings.

My mom couldn't tell if it was a man under the coverings or a woman, but the person had the same eyes as Regan from The Exorcist. They were drooling from the mouth, emitting a low growl, heavy breathing, and all that.

My mom says that "uncanny valley feeling" came upon her, and the other Soldiers and the TCP let them go on their way. No VBIED attacks in the AO happened, but my mom (or whoever she was talking about) said they would never forget those eyes for the rest of their life.

Cults Of Iraq

Back in 2009, the Executive Officer (XO) at a Forward Operating Base (FOB) asked me to report on the cultures and history. That FOB encompassed and protected an ancient ziggurat. Not sure why. Much of the sectarian stuff was disturbing fringe stuff, so maybe they were trying to figure things out. They were also interested in the small Jewish population as well.

The weird stuff usually centered around a single dude, a mystic that focused on the darker stuff. Mystic Islam isn't about the Quran as much as the spiritual connection. Honestly looks closer to Hinduism than Islam in that way. Meditation, narcotics, trances, and rituals to summon or "become one with" whatever. The mystic ones focus that energy on the Jinn, Iblis, etc.

I tried to find more info (I couldn't keep the report I did), but Google sucks for research now. All that will pop up is the Yazidis which have their baddies too. They focus on Marduk. A couple of things if you want to dig into it. Physical evidence shows that Zoroastrianism does not pre-date Judaism. It just predates the Jewish exile to

Babylon. Also, Islam is a relatively new religion. These are super important details because the diffusion of ancient cultures ties all the boogie men origin stories together. One of these days, I'll get back into it. The stories that pop out when you have all that info are engrossing.

For instance, an Islamic fighter created a brigade of extremists (as in too fucked up for other extremists to associate with) that would kill their enemies and eat their hearts and/or livers. This way, they destroy their opposition and gain the power and knowledge of the person they killed. They validate this from a story where Hind ate the liver of Hamzeh, the companion of the Prophet Muhammad.

Those guys still considered themselves Muslims. You also have the counter culture guys, who see Islam as a corruption of an older (better or more powerful religion). Cryptids, Jinn, Ghouls, etc., are all whisperings of religions of the past. Usually, ancient holdover pieces blending local and foreign beliefs. Inevitably some crazy with a dark past latches on to this stuff and tries to revive it.

He is given or finds some "secret" knowledge that ties together with whatever ancient mystery he wants to use to validate whatever he's selling. The MO of these guys is always the same. They seek validation, pleasure, influence, and power. When they focus on the darker spirits, things get sick. I call these guys anti-Muslims. They get off on doing all the things Islam says are evil. They do rituals to summon these Jinn beings (these guys are pretty much the same worldwide, Strigoi, Fairy, etc.).

These anti-Muslim guys want to channel these spirits to help them fight their enemies. They like the ones that target travelers and strangers (i.e. us), these Jinns are usually extra spooky. So these guys focus on connecting with that shit. Now throw in a combat zone. Various people stacking bodies on the regular for generations in a consolidated area. It's no wonder our guys see freaky stuff.

Memories Of The Old Regime

Not incredibly spooky, but here's my story—middle of Baghdad. The Army has fallen in on many buildings that belonged to Saddam. We are posted up across from the former Ba'ath Party HQ. I'm not sure what this building I'm in used to be, but I know the ones around me belonged to the Republican Guard. Some of these buildings still had legit torture chambers in them.

My spotter thought he heard me call him and laugh like clear as day. Like I was going to show him something funny and he came into the room but I wasn't there. It's happened to him twice with the voices of guys in our team. It's also happened to another dude in our team who woke up screaming loud as hell every other night.

The Bear Remained In The Mountains

I don't really believe in ghosts, but I got creeped out one night in northeastern Afghanistan, and to this day, I'm still not sure what to think.

We had conducted this massive operation to push into a valley that was Taliban controlled and establish an outpost on what the locals called Russian Hill. The story went that during their invasion, a battalion of Russian Soldiers had been overrun and slaughtered on the hill. They were tortured and dismembered up there.

It took us a week to reach the hill, with Troops In Contact (TIC) each day leading to it. We finally reached it and had to have a Mine Clearing Linge Charge (MCLC) clear a path up to it as Russian mines still surrounded it. We quickly established hasty fighting positions and began digging in.

Afghan Army Soldiers with us refused to go up the hill, so they set up at the base. They were seriously freaked. That night, we heard screams and footsteps around the mountain. The screams sounded distant yet right outside the perimeter. The footsteps sounded like they were right next to us.

As I said, I have no idea what the fuck it was, and I don't really believe in ghosts or spirits, but especially given the context of where we were and the fact that people were trying to kill us every day, it was freaky as fuck. We thought it was Taliban fucking with us, and it may very well have been.

In a previous TIC (not part of this operation), they got so close we were trading hand grenades. During that, they yelled obscenities to us. Some were in broken English. But it seriously sounded like the screams were very close, and the footsteps couldn't be explained. I don't know man could have just as quickly been our delirious state. Several of us heard it.

The Giant Of Kunar

I was deployed as an infantry team leader with the Army in the Kunar province of Afghanistan from 2008 to 2009. One night we set in on an observation patrol to overlook a village that we suspected IEDs were coming out of due to a successful IED recovery a few weeks prior. My lieutenant gave me a new thermal imaging system called the Recon3 that none of us were familiar with and told me to figure out what I can and pass along that information to the other team leaders. I started messing with the Recon3 to see its capabilities and was surprised at the clarity of the zoom on it. I spent most of my time messing with the different functionalities and watching the village.

I started to look across the valley to what I could see and that led me to look along the spur we were set in on and saw a very large heat signature at the top of one of the false peaks. I did everything I could to get as clear of an image as I could, suspecting that it was a group of Taliban huddled together around a light as they tend to do in the mountains. All of the sudden, the heat signature stood up as one being. The trees in that area grew up to about 10 to 12 ft tall, and this thing was at least as tall, if not taller than the trees that surrounded it. It started taking steps parallel to my position and was covering ground quickly with ease. Its stride was slow and relaxed, yet it moved with incredible speed. That led me to believe that this creature was gigantic.

It very quickly traversed the landscape, and I lost sight of it along a neighboring spur. I did not believe what I saw initially, assuming I had imagined it. I never had seen anything like that in my life.

I didn't tell many people about it, while I was in and even when I got out. I kept it to myself, thinking there was no way I saw what I saw. But then in 2010, I listened to a story on Coast to Coast… specifically the story about the Giant of Kandahar. That made all the memories of my time in service come flooding back and made me consider other things I saw during that deployment.

For instance, the creature was described as having fire orange hair and it reminded me of a tradition the locals in the area of my sighting would do. They would die their hair a bright orange color and even would dye their goats the same color. They never gave any explanation why. It seemed like it was every once in a while they would do this, and then all of the sudden those orange dyed goats would be gone, and the local's hair would also no longer be dyed orange. I assumed maybe it was a cultural thing I didn't understand, but now it makes me wonder if that was some kind of gesture to the creature/Nephilim or the goats were sacrificed to it.

I am a Christian, and the bible briefly discussed the "Men of Renown," aka the Nephilim. I think that's what I saw, a member of an ancient race of giants that descended from fallen angels. Or it could be something like Sasquatch. I'm not sure.

Ghosts In The Ruins Of Samarra

I had participated with the Invasion of Iraq, back in 2003 as an Abrams Crewmember in the US Army. We marched all the way north to Mosul, then turned around and headed back to Samarra, where we finally set up a permanent FOB.

Near Samarra were the incredibly ancient ruins, of the Spiral Minaret and the Golden Mosque (later destroyed by ISIS). The ruins were incredible, and even though I was never able to actually walk through there and check it out, we patrolled nearby to make sure everything was quiet.

One time filling in for a gunner's position, we were scanning the ruins at night, to look for any obvious hot spots of Insurgents. Some of the stones in these ruins still retained residual heat from the hot sun, so they would produce a glow on our IR sites.

This only happened a few times, and was reported by several tank crews, as well as our Scouts with their LRS trucks. But sometimes when scanning the ruins, there were cold spots moving through the ruins, and in between the burial sites at the nearby mausoleum. These would show up, clear as day on our powerful main gun

16

sights, but there were no bodies, objects or anything like that. Just incredibly cold spots moving around slowly, through the ruins, moving in front and behind stones. It was the weirdest thing I remember seeing on that deployment, and we still never really got an answer to what was going on.

UFOs Over Taji Iraq

Tank Commander on an Abrams M1A2 SEP MBT, and my platoon and I (four Abrams) were spread out about 1000m along MSR Tampa to keep an eye on the convoys. It's probably around 0300 in the morning, and I have my entire crew get some sleep, while I stay up monitoring the CITV.

While doing a routine scan, I see a light up in the sky that's brighter than anything else I can see that night. It pops up in the CITV, and I can see it with my own eyes. I have the tank running on battery power, so there's no noise from the turbine, and the CITV doesn't require hydraulics so it's also silent. Whatever this thing was, it made no noise. It hovered in place, probably 3-400m out, moved around a bit, then just took off super-fast. I never really felt threatened by it, just super curious. This was 2006, so personal drones weren't really a thing in small Iraqi villages, and the only drones we had at the time were incredibly loud, and couldn't just hover in place.

I talked to my platoon about it, and no one else saw anything, and chalked it all up to lack of sleep, stress and dehydration. They could be right, but it certainly seemed real to me, whatever the hell it was.

Vietnam Now

So, my father was in Vietnam and saw some crazy shit. One base he was on (which he won't tell me the name of since it's no longer there, and he doesn't want me to try and look it up and accidentally end up on a watch list) was a sweet assignment. My Dad had to work in an office, fix copiers or printers and sort random nonsense paper. He said he got picked out to be sent there and that it was an easy assignment.

So he's in this small base with about 100 other guys. All sorts of people all again picked out to be stationed here. They used to come up with stories and jokes about why there were sent there. But it was cool at first, they would party and have fun. Typical old school Army shenanigans. My dad worked with a crew of about 12-15 other guys. None of the papers made any sense. The only way they could sort them was by a number at the top. Some were things like the types of certain flowers. Some didn't even make any sense at all, and were like word vomit.

They would get boxes and boxes of these papers to sort every day via a big truck. They didn't have a quota or really anyone telling them what to do, so they usually worked 6-8 hours. They would call it quits for the night. Around two or so months in, they would start to experience something that became a regular phenomenon. My dad said he woke up one morning to everything in his room shaking. Like he in the middle of an earthquake. When he went outside, everyone was out looking around. My dad asked a few guys what they were looking for, and one of the guys said they saw something big fly over the base.

My dad thought maybe it was a bomber or something, so he brushed them off. After that, they had regular earthquakes to the point where they wouldn't react anymore. At night they started to see lights and colors flash outside their windows, and they would hear noises if they were outside alone, night or day. A few guys got spooked and would request to be reassigned. One by one, guys who were usually chill and laid back would snap and become panicked shells of themselves.

One night my dad is outside when he hears what sounds like running. Like someone in full sprint but all around him. Like it was everywhere he looked, but he was just missing seeing what was running. He tossed a cigarette away and started to walk off. He started to hear what sounded like a squeaking noise behind him, and began to be filled with pure dread. More than he has felt in his life. Like he knew he was about to die. Luckily the tossed cigarette caught a patch of dried grass on fire. He snapped out of it once he saw fire spreading, and ran to grab an extinguisher. But when he came back it was daylight, and people were out. Looking for him. He had been missing for four hours. It felt like minutes to my dad.

Not long after, another guy went crazy and set a building on fire. Big trucks showed up, and my dad and the others left that base. Well, my dad was as bit of a shithead, and decided to go AWOL with a few others and find that base. He said when he reached the area, the entire place was an overgrown field. Like nothing had been there before. My dad couldn't explain it. But in the following years everyone who he spoke to couldn't tell him about that base. Just my dad and the handful of others there with him.

Al Anbar Burning Bush

The story you posted about Al Anbar 2018; I was there as well. Now I don't think this story qualifies as haunted, supernatural, or anything like that. But to this day, I have no explanation for what I saw, and you might get a kick out of it.

Now plenty of boys had ghost stories around camp that their posts were haunted. Packs of wild dogs roamed freely throughout the base. Some of these dogs were big mean-looking fuckers. Most of them were starved, but there were also ones that were well fed. The point is, there was enough reason to be on your toes walking around at night. Anyway, here's my story: I was lucky enough to pull the night shift nearly the whole deployment, and I was glad for it. The days were hotter than fuck.

Well, on this night, on a post that had become a second home to me, I saw something. For orientation, I will say the camp had about 600 meters of open desert in front of it without obstruction.

There was a road running across the frontage at nearly the 600 mark. Now I stress this detail because I want you to understand that by this time in the deployment, I know every square inch of that 600-meter frontage. It's pitch black and quiet as always when suddenly I see the light. Not a vehicle light on the road, which occasionally happened. This was a low glow and much closer than the road. My initial thought is it's a headlamp.

I figured some Iraqi Soldier was moving outside their post. But it was much too close. Maybe 4-500 meters. And there were never Iraqis closer than the road. We had no shortage of optics, I had ta thermal scope on hand, and I looked into the desert. Not a person, but a small smoking bush. A bush was on fire. It was much clearer on thermals. But there was nobody and nothing else around it. It

19

was a small bush. Like the kind you trip over running Range 410.

I scan the desert for any nearby movement but nothing. I stare into the thermals relentlessly. This is the most exciting thing to happen on the post in months. Eventually, the smoldering bush calms. Now I am confused but not overly excited. Yet. Suddenly I notice a new glow. Maybe 250 meters to the right of the last and closer. But there is no one and nothing around it to have started it. I'm not the only one who sees it. Another guy on duty confirms what I see, although he is much less interested.

This continues for the next few hours. One flame goes out. Another starts in a different location. These are sparse desert weeds at least 6-10 meters apart. The fires start hundreds of meters apart and there was no wind. The distance between the flames was too far and random to be natural transference. To this day, I have no idea how these fires started. Spontaneous combustion? Who knows?

Through The CROW

Afghanistan July 2020 at CL Dwyer. We had towers from 0000-0800. My friend and I were on tower two that watched over the ECP lane. Some other guys from my platoon also had similar experiences to mine.

We always took turns sleeping, so he's knocked out. On my crow system, I could see a black blob on the CROW, moving along the concrete walls, just floating.

It only lasted a couple of seconds, but I put my NVGs on and went outside to see if anyone was on the lane coming towards the tower, and no one was there.

That was the first time I had ever seen the CROW system act up like that, so I don't know if it was a malfunction or just something weird.

Strangely enough, my friend had a weird experience in that tower: "[ANON], and I were sitting in the tower, our radio started making pig noises and just freaking out, and then the CROW started charging on its own, and the screen was changing colors and going black very fast, and then the screen just stayed one solid color, and the gun kept charging."

Guardian Angel

In 03 (OIF1), a terrible sand storm was coming in. I had been standing guard at an OP all night, so I was getting some rest in one of those big tents. It was just all the OP guys in that tent, but I was the only one in that tent sleeping. Everybody else was at the guard shack or on an OP.

While I was sleeping, I was violently shaken awake by two hands on both sides of my body. A voice said to leave the tent. I opened the flap to the tent, to a very windy horrible sand storm rolling in hardcore.

A few seconds later, the big wooden beams that held the tent up collapsed. I would have been crushed by one of those beams if I hadn't been woken up. I believe it was an angel.

I know there are probably some hardcore folks on here that don't believe in God, hate God, but it was real. Curious if anyone else has a similar story while on deployment.

Tree People

My husband served in Vietnam from 1970-71. He and others saw what they called Tree Spirits in Vietnam.

Tree spirits are Soldiers who died fighting in Vietnam. My husband said you could see shadows that looked like Soldiers with weapons. He said you could distinguish the shadows if they were Vietcong, NVA, and even American Soldiers.

Perhaps guarding the area? He didn't think these spirits knew they were dead. The night sky would light up with artillery illumination rounds and he would see them in the trees.

Miles

My dad's late friend Miles used to be in a recon battalion in Vietnam. He saw some messed-up stuff because they were usually alone and way ahead of everyone. He told me that once and a while, you'd see people at night, like silhouettes in the trees, bushes, and grass.

He described a few of them as black, and others as "Predator" like see through. But because they are in the thick of it, anything could mean the enemy so they acted accordingly. But nothing would phase these things. You'd shoot but they would just stand and stare.

Miles used to tell me that he believed the government was doing experiments out there or the land was cursed. He also believed that that they were ghosts who couldn't leave the field so they would just wait and watch. Miles was a crazy bastard even up until his death. But when it came to Vietnam, he was dead serious and swore he wasn't lying.

Afghan UFOs

In Afghanistan, I saw lights flying around way faster than anything humans make. My platoon had a video of it once, and I've been trying to hunt it down, but no one seems to have it anymore, which breaks my heart because it was trippy. I've been trying to hunt down that video since 2012.

They were the same thing you see from the F-18 videos on FLIR. But they were dancing around on the mountain tops near Kandahar looking East.

Usually, two or three at a time, started slowly hovering on the ridgeline, crisscrossing, then speeding up, and abruptly stopping. Defying all physics. I remember me and a team leader just standing there while on patrol watching them.

I even called it up to our company and told them. They didn't see it I guess. We watched for a few more minutes, and then it just took off straight up. Even more oddly, we just picked up and continued to walk on patrol like it never even happened.

Honestly, it was too far off to say if it was tic-tac shape or not, and it was nighttime through NVGs, but most likely. Saw it two or three times over eight months in Afghanistan.

Vietnam

I don't know all the terminology he used, but I will tell you the best I can. Dad was in the 101st Airborne and carried an M60. So, I guess you could call him the big gun, I think. He would start by saying that it was a rainy night. He said you could set the time on watch by the rain on most days. Then there were times it would rain for days.

Well, during one of the times when it had been raining for days, he said he had been posted on the camp's perimeter as security (there may be some details here I'm missing that military folks may understand). He said it had gotten dark, and the rain was relentless. There was almost continuous lightning.

He was seated behind a fallen tree with his M60 pointing into the darkness over the tree as it was perched on its tripod. After a bit of time sitting in the rain and lightning, he heard movement in front of him.

Before he could notify anyone else, he said a giant gorilla rushed him. He said he could see the lightning flashes as it came at him.

He said he then opened fire on it, hitting it several times. After all the commotion was over, there was no gorilla to be found, only blood on the ground.

He swore what he saw was a giant gorilla. I remember him telling me this story before I heard anything about the "Rock Ape" stories.

Bari Alai

The OP was Bari Alai, notably the first time the Taliban successfully overran a US outpost in the war. We retook it and held it with a company-sized element. We significantly improved it by airlifting (no road access) better weapons and supplies, among other notable improvements.

One night, I was doing what I did best, stirring our waste with JP8 until it was burned to ash and could be disposed of off the mountainside. Now, when I say the midnight sky was clear, it was breathtakingly clear. One by one, until three arrived, lights not much larger than stars appeared in the heavens. Two were star-like blue, but one was red. Nothing odd right away.

However, they began to rapidly and independently dart, and even more eerily, stop and change direction completely. No man-made platform could move at this comet-like speed, dead stop, and ultimately change direction. It was more fascinating than eerie, but it made you feel insignificant in that midnight dark mountainous valley.

Something Big

Guard shift 0100. Myself and another private staring into the dark abyss of the Kunar River valley below. The glow of NVGs reflecting on our eye our only light. Our shack is 8x8 made of plywood, barely strong enough to hold the anti-mortar single sandbag layer on the roof. Metallica quietly plays on a speaker.

Many sightings of large creatures had happened in the mountains, some even taller than us. Always through thermals and always far, far away, and blurry. Tonight, was different.

Something big jumped onto the side of our guard shack and latched on with claws. It climbed to our roof as a large cat would, right up a vertical face. There was some creaking from the added weight. It jumped down into the dark and was not seen again.

Afghanistan Skinwalker Part I

So, it starts with my dad, he is on watch in a deserted village top facing a mountain. He and his group are situated at a wall overlooking the village. Along with this village, there is a wall. Now, this wall has doors leading into small square spaces, which were most likely homes. This wall was about roughly 30 to 40 feet keep in mind.

So, my dad is mounted on this wall look down the alley they are situated on. He has a 50-caliber turret of some kind. I can't recall what he said, but I do know it was a 50 caliber. He's also got NVGs, and other night seeing equipment. Sorry if I don't know all the correct terms for this. But he is sitting there on that wall, and he sees a man walking down the mountain about 500 meters from his group.

This is unusual because it's 0200-0300 in the morning, and there is just a man casually walking around this abandoned village at two in the morning. So, he sees him and starts closely watching him. He says that the man sees him, looks at him, then keeps walking. But he is walking weirdly and gets on all fours and turns into a whole panther. He thought he was sleep-deprived since they had spent all night driving to get there. But he has rubbed his eyes, and he's trying to wake up his buddy he called Cooter, as well as his First Sergeant since this was his first deployment.

So, he's throwing these discarded caliber rounds at his group, and they aren't waking up. He looked back through his NVG scope or something and saw this thing jump onto the wall. When it jumped on the wall, it was about 60-100 meters away from him. So he started yelling, his guys woke up, and he told them what he saw, and they were laughing at him and telling him he just saw things, but he knew what he saw and stood by it. The next night it's Cooters turn, and he sees the same thing, but it gets closer. So Cooter woke up my dad and said that he saw it and said he was freaking out, and he finally knew he was serious.

Afghanistan Skinwalker Part II
Dad's first-hand account

We were in Logar province in the mountains of Pule Alam (not sure on the spelling). It was 2013, we were embedded with an ANA BN doing operations to clear small towns of insurgents. We parked for the night in an old unfinished, but what looked to be some housing area.

I had the night shift watch on the M2 and had an AN/PAS 13 thermal sight. It was about 0300. I saw a heat signature of a person at the end of the road, which was only 150 meters. I kept my eye on this dude. He was walking straight towards our small AA.

He started moving to my left. He was still 80 meters away from us. He turned into a small alley, but I was elevated high enough in the truck I could still see him. He stopped for what seemed like an hour but was only five minutes—looking around and moving his hands in an odd manner. He started walking out of the alley and got down on all fours, and moved about 20 meters that way before he turned into an enormous cat.

At this time, he was about 50 meters or less from where we were bedded down. I started throwing expended 50 cal rounds and yelling at my dudes to wake up. My buddy Cooter woke up and saw this thing coming towards them, grabbed his rifle and started yelling. It came as close as 15 feet from the guys sleeping on the ground. After Cooter started yelling, this thing ran off and hid in one of the buildings that was in the area.

The very next night, Cooter was on guard and around the same time, it happened again exactly the way I explained it. Except for this time, it got closer, and everyone else got a good look at it. It was black and quite large. It was just a big huge black cat.

It was like the size of a tiger, maybe a little smaller. We could hear it breathing super weird. I thought for sure I was going crazy. I was trying to explain it away to myself that I didn't really see that happen. But after my buddy saw the same thing, I knew what I saw.

A Test Of Faith At FOB Iskandiriyah

This goes back to 2006, my first deployment to Iraq at FOB Iskandiriyah. Our schedule was one week Tower Guard, one-week QRF, and one-week patrols from our patrol base in Jurf As Sakr. This particular event happened when I was on Tower Guard with a buddy of mine. Everyone knows that everything under the sun comes up on guard. This time, it was Christianity and Faith.

He's a devout Christian, as was his father. We delved pretty deep into the Faith, the Bible, and what his father had taught him... Several hours into our conversation, I had to take a piss. I climbed down out of the Tower and headed over to the Porto John. I want to add because I know people will say it held sway over my psyche: I, at no point in time, was thinking about anything other than taking a piss. Also, there was a street light shining over the area in question.

Anyway, as I stepped out of the pisser and started walking towards the Tower, I heard a noise from my right to left. I paused, thinking, what was that? As I took another few steps forward, I heard it from my left to right. I followed that with my eyes... I looked up at the sky, wondering if maybe it was sprinkling or wind or whatever. This time, as I walked forward towards the Tower, I watched the ground. I followed the "scuttling" sound from my right to left with my eyes. It sounded like claws "scuttling" across the ground, yet all I could do was follow the sound. It sounded like claws running across the asphalt, like five feet away from me.

I lost it, haha. Hair on the back of the neck, shortness of breath... All that. I rushed up the ladder and told my buddy. As calm as he always was, he says... "Yea bro... that happens when you get deep into the Bible.". He said his dad had shit like that happen to him. He said things happen. They get active whenever you get deep into the Bible. They try to scare you away from it. The first time it crossed my path, I half-ass noticed it.

The Russian

So I was deployed to Afghanistan for a year. My job had me traveling all over the country, so I could never really settle in for too long. We stayed a few weeks in Bagram at one of the many camps around the airfield. As soon as I settled into this room, I was uneasy. It looked as if whoever previously lived there had left in a hurry with a few personal belongings scattered throughout the room. There was a negative vibe in general. I just shrugged it off as post-mission jitters and figured that person was sent home early for something.

That first night, I couldn't help but feel something was watching me, and that's not a feeling you like when you're all alone in a strange room inside a warzone. I finally forced myself to sleep and began having a strange dream over and over again. In the dream, I walked into a dark room dimly lit with candles laid out in a circle surrounding this podium. On the podium sat a ledger book with a quill and ink bottle.

I walked up to the podium and began writing something. It was then that I felt a large hand press down on my right shoulder as if it was a person trying to wake me up. I woke up from that nightmare so quickly that I almost hit my head on the unoccupied bunk above me. I looked over, and a large man was wearing a soviet Russian uniform, and AK was standing next to my bed.

His head was obscured from view (due to the bunk just above me), and he looked as if he was trying to pull me out of bed. I reactively swung at him, thinking that I was about to go hand to hand with an AK-wielding man in my bedroom, only to throw myself into the floor in a gasping panic. He had disappeared into nothing. I immediately thought I was going crazy and went back to bed.

The next few days, I would see things thrown across my room, hear voices speaking at night (Russian and Afghan), and continue having the same dream over and over again. The worst part was that no one believed me until my LT saw a Febreze bottle fly across my room.

Just A Set Of Footprints

Was at COP near Ramadi. I was standing post from 0000-0800, the worst shift out there. We're in position one facing westward. From the edge of our wire, it's an open desert for a couple of clicks until there's an abandoned grouping of buildings and a cemetery.

Around 0300, I let my buddy on post snooze off for a bit, and I'm scanning out sector with my NVGs from right to left. As I scan back across to my right, there's suddenly a dude standing about 300m to my direct front. I don't know where he came from because it's kilometers of open terrain for him to pop up out of nowhere. I wake up my buddy, and he sees the guy and tags him with his PEQ15 so we can give an area to the other post and the COC's GBOSS.

As he's doing that, I pick up the PAS13 (thermal scope) to see what else is happening around him. I don't pick him up at all. I end up looking through my NVGs with one eye and the thermal with the other. We both see the dude on canvas, not on thermal. We shine one of those bright asses surefire 10,000-lumen lights and see nothing. But still, see him with NVGs.

28

We call up COC to report it all to the SOG, and they're getting the same thing. SOG gathers up a fire team and patrols out to investigate. They've got eyes on under NVGs, and as they come out of a draw about 50m from the dude, he's gone all of a sudden. We lost the guy on our NVGs as the team came out of the draw.

SOG comes back says he found a set of footprints. Just stationary like no trails leading to or from the spot. It was as if the dude had walked up and stopped. But no prints leading to or from the area. Just two solitary prints. If it were just me who saw it, I'd chalk it up to sleep deprivation. But eight other people saw it. So I'm guessing it was a fucking ghost or the most ninja insurgent to walk the earth.

Shadows In The Bush

I deployed in Africa. My base had gotten attacked about a few weeks prior, so we were working every day, so I was exhausted. one night, I was in my tower sitting down, and I felt a human hand grab my shoulder and shake. I freak out and turn around (we were in blackout, mind you). See nothing. I look through my NVGs and thermals, and I can't find anything. For more context, I worked nights the whole time. That place was naturally creepy at night hyenas, bugs, snakes, all that.

It was much more than an aggressive shake. It was also hot and humid at night, but when this happened, I felt the temperature noticeably get cold. I'm not superstitious, but that did feel like something not ordinary. Additionally, my buddy had a nearly identical experience in the same tower on a separate night. For reference, this is a tower about 20ft or so off the ground. The only way up is a ladder. If anyone did climb up there, you would have heard them on the aluminum ladder.

Some of my buddies also had some weird experiences out there. One guy thought he saw someone climbing the fence, but it could only be seen through the thermals, which was pretty odd because only one guy saw it without thermals, a shadow figure of sorts. The real creepy one, though, was a friend who said he saw someone walk out of the wood line and look at him. Like same as before, this shadowy figure was just staring him down. He felt it was a security risk. He and a few others drew weapons. But before anyone said anything, this figure disappears in thin air.

Black Triangle Over Iraq

I did 16 months in Iraq with the Army back in '06- '07. My company was split between several COPs along MSR Tampa. One night my buddy and I were pulling guard duty out of a bunker on top of a hill that our outpost was built around. We were sitting there talking and doing our scans of the perimeter and surrounding area. We had NVGs and the thermal scope from a CLU.

It wasn't uncommon to see Blackhawks flying by and the occasional AC-130, and we knew other planes were flying much higher regularly. As I was scanning with my NVGs, something in the air caught my eye, and I looked up to see a huge dark triangular-shaped craft moving slowly towards and then over our base.

I alerted my buddy, who also saw it through NVGs. He grabbed the thermals, and this thing gave off no discernible heat signature. It was a dark area moving above us, blocking out stars when we looked with our naked eyes. No lights, no sound. It never stopped moving, just a slow and steady pace.

It was impossible to tell how high it was since depth perception is tricky with NVGs. Judging its size was hard too, but it was bigger than anything you usually see flying. I've looked up flying black triangles online, and there are stories out there of things like this. It was not a B2 bomber, way sharper angles to the triangle, and not an F117 either, as it was just a three-sided triangle.

STATESIDE

The Growl

So I graduated AIT and came to Fort Stewart around late 2019, and I never experienced anything paranormal my entire life. I was in sleeping in my room one day, and I woke up and heard a growl.

As I heard the growl, something pushed my bed, and something was on top of me on my chest. I didn't see what was on top of me because I slept with a blanket over my face. I tried to get up, and I only got up once, but then whatever was on top of my chest put more pressure on me, and it was getting hard to breathe.

I tried to say, get off me, but I legit couldn't get a word out, so I just laid there and started praying so it can leave me alone. This thing sounded like it started talking to me as I was praying. I think it said it wouldn't help, but I don't remember. After my prayer, everything was normal, and I could breathe again. Crazy as I never experienced anything paranormal my entire life.

Yakima Sasquatch

I think this a Bigfoot sighting.

Yakima Training Center, 2017. Setting up a TA. Late at night on security in a gun truck, and my driver swears he sees a dude running around through the CROWs. This is the middle of nowhere Washington State, nobody is around for miles except us, and we weren't expecting OPFOR.

My driver gets a closer look and its fuzzy, but clearly something walking around on two legs like a human. I go outside to take a piss away from the truck and I hear this god-awful yowl in the distance. My driver yells from the truck to me to get back inside. When I get back inside he says he saw the thing on the CROWs let out that yowl and look right in my direction.

I didn't get out the of the truck that night.

Fort Meyer

I was a Private in the Old Guard up until Sergeant. It's not shocking that a base adjacent / connected to Arlington National Cemetery, which has 400,000 deceased, would be haunted. You knew the base was haunted. Two companies were decimated in Vietnam, but you won't find any history about Foxtrot or Golf company. You would hear lockers slamming, shadows, nothing too, too bad.

Two of the creepiest stories I have are this: one night, my runner and I were hanging around the Delta Company CQ desk on the last two-hour leg of the shift. Suddenly, we hear someone walking down the side steps, which was unusual, wearing the ceremonial shoes called "steels." It's very distinctive, like tap shoes.

Suddenly, an entirely ceremonial dressed Old Guard Soldier is walking in front of us, but we can see through him to the other hallway. He's walking as if heading out to a funeral with a rifle. He was in the old uniform that had the long service Stripes.

As soon as he's about midway to the door, he disappears. I turn to my runner and say, "you saw that right." The kid looks at me like, "fuck yes, I saw that." It wasn't uncommon to see strange things, especially by section 7A, where lights or orbs were seen A LOT. 7A is in the middle of the cemetery, far away from any actual lights.

One night, another time I'm doing CQ, I head downstairs to lay on one of the couches in the command hallways. Old Guard companies are like U-shaped frat houses. The top is the PLT off-post rooms. Mid floors are barracks, and basements are CPs. So I'm lying down on this couch reading a book, and I can FEEL someone watching me at the end of a long hallway that just turns black. Like Venta Black.

As I look up (getting chills), this dark figure turns and walks down to the other side of the hallway—a complete outline of a tall Soldier. I lift my book and go, "whatever." This ghost wanted my attention because it came right to the edge of the light, so the next time, it was right up on me.

Seeing these things often, I raised my book again and said, "go away, I'm not in the mood." After that, the feeling of being watched lifted. Besides the new barracks, all the old companies have this feeling. Like I said. Being attached to an ANC, it's not uncommon to see many strange things.

Fort Sill

US Army Vet: In April 1996, I arrived at Ft. Sill, Ok, and was assigned to the MP company working out of a correctional facility. On my first night there, I was given a barracks room in this old building and felt strange while I was there. I had nothing, just the military gear I traveled with, no TV or radio.

I unpacked and prepared my uniform for the next day off in-processing, shined my boots, and decided to go to bed. I woke up at some point in the night, and there floating at eye level while lying in my bed, I saw this small Indian! He had his hair pulled back into a ponytail, large, and, I mean, large black eyes and was looking at me blinking.

I started to sit up, and he floated into my face going " La, La, La" (like you would hear Indian calls on a movie). I took a swing at it, and it floated back, then as my hand went by, it did it again, "La, La, La!" I thought I had to be dreaming, so I jumped up and rubbed my eyes. When I stopped, I was standing up, and nothing was there.

Not sure if I should tell anyone, I did say to another Soldier when I arrived at the prison and was taking a tour, he and a couple of others had the same sighting their first night. I was told that the MP barracks there was an Indian Hospital back in the day, and Geronimo died there.

Sure enough, just outside the front doors is a marker on a large boulder stating this was an Indian Hospital, and he did die there. Several months later, my in-laws were visiting, and we went to an Indian museum on the post and as I walked around the place.

I came upon a painting of a group of Indians dancing around a campfire, and in the puffs of smoke were those little Indians I saw that night. The plaque said something like an Indian demon dance to keep spirits out of the camp. Some 25 years later, I still have a hard time at night by myself. My kids get a kick out of this every time I tell it. But it has freaked me out, and I have never received an answer to what it was.

Skinwalker On Fort Hood

We were occupying a range on Fort Hood and bivouacked at a nearby OP. We had all gone to sleep and our set up amounted to a gypsy camp. I was asleep in my hammock when I was awakened by a Soldier wearing ACU's (this was right at the time of the wear out date so it wasn't too unusual). I looked at him a bit disoriented from waking up and he stared at me spoking in complete gibberish. The next morning, I awoke and told my battle buddies about what I thought was a weird dream.

They all proceeded to tell me not only had they come in contact with this unknown Soldier but he also tried communicating with them. My first buddy proceeded to say how a trooper in ACU's woke him up and asked him to follow the unknown Soldier into the supply tent, my buddy being super agitated at being woken up, told him to fuck off and went back to sleep. Another Soldier stated something tried to violently enter his tent for a few minutes.

A third Soldier chimed in and said he was awoken by the ruckus and witnessed a figure in ACU's walk into the tree line and none of us saw him again. We all believed it was a Skinwalker and a part of one of many curses on Fort Hood. We told one of the contractors for the range and not only did he believe it but he pointed to spots on the map that were considered tribal land and said that was a fairly common occurrence.

"We heard the bootsteps"

I was stationed at Fort Lewis, Washington State, back in 1984. I worked in the computer room for the 9th infantry Division. I started work roughly at 0200. I was the only one in the building. This building was a common converted old barracks. Two stories, a long building with a restroom at one end. The computer room was downstairs at the other end of the building from the latrine.

One night I was running my programs blasting the loud music (80's music), and everything was normal.

I hear boot steps upstairs—heavy boot steps like the sound of jump boots. The steps started at the opposite end of the building and stopped above the computer room. Being the curious young Soldier, I went upstairs to see who came in early. This was 0230ish. I looked upstairs and no lights were on. I turned on the lights and went upstairs. I checked everywhere I did not see a soul. I went back to the computer room and went about my business. I did not feel creeped out or afraid.

I told my NCO the following day. They said it was the building settling. I know the difference between a building settling and boot steps; but decided not to pursue it any further. Again, I was very comfortable with the situation. I would occasionally hear the boot steps but just ignored them. Months later, I had a recruit working the shift with me so I could train him. Sure enough, we heard the boot steps. The new guy was creeped out by it. Me being a smartass, I cranked the music loud. I told him, let's piss off the ghosts.

Then the boot steps stopped right above us and we heard a loud bang. As if a desk was turned over on its side, right above us. So I say let's go check it out. I went upstairs, nothing was out of place. By this time, the new guy was freaked out.

He said at least we are safe locked in the computer room. I told him it's a ghost. They can walk through walls. After that, the new guy was too freaked to work the graveyard shift with me. I just wish I knew what I know now about ghosts. I would have stayed up there and tried to talk to them. I believe those buildings have since been torn down.

The Tall Man

Nothing exciting: we'd set up a patrol base in a wood line at the bottom of a decent size hill. This was mid Covid19 lockdown, and the chain of command had decided that sentries would still go out in pairs but would have to be spaced two meters apart. The way the ground fell on my section's position meant that I might as well have been by myself. It was too far to even whisper without someone hearing you, so we mostly kept to ourselves.

About halfway through my shift, I saw a shadowy figure stand up at the top of the hill. I was tempted to call a stand-to, but I noticed he wasn't armed and in any military gear (no helmet/webbing/armor, etc.). Eventually, I blinked, and he was gone. It was just a silhouette of a very tall man, it was dark out, and I couldn't make out any clothing/facial detail whatsoever

About five minutes later, he appears again, 1/3 of the way down, then vanishes again. A few minutes later, he's 2/3s down the hill. He's definitely, not military. At this point, I'm praying he doesn't come any closer because I don't want to deal with whatever it is, natural or supernatural. But after that time I don't see him anymore. I talked to the guy the same time as me the next day, and he never saw anything, so I'm 99% sure it was just me. Hallucinations or something else? I'm not sure.

Big Cat At Benning

So, back when 3BDE HBCT was a thing, we used to do field training between un-stabilized and stabilized gunnery (Wheeled and Tracked Gunnery). So, somewhere between Table X and XII, we had a combined arms mission. I, along with two other dudes, got sent out on an overnight operation. Kind of recon but primarily to probe enemy village/force. It is the mock-up village in the F ranges near Darby.

It has a big ole swamp on West Side that runs N to S, and the village is on a hill crest about 250' above it on a slow roll up a knoll. Anyway, there is a well-worn dirt road that leads East-West from the village to a lake, then SW to Darby.

We got dropped off on the far West Side of the swamp, I think it was F-23, and we had to trek 2.3 km to target on F19. I have deer hunted that area religiously. The boundary fence was south of us about a 1 km. Anyway, we were in ghillie suits and following a dirt path till we hit the road. It's 2300 and a bright ass full moon, so we can see everything without NVGs.

We hit that E/W road, and we hear something like walking. So we skirt the road and hide on the north side. There we waited, listened, nothing. So we move on and about 800 more meters we hit a checkpoint, and we still hear movement. So we wait, still waiting. I got annoyed and walked down to the road.

In a dead tree is a big, black spot. I remove my nod and look at it. Still there, highlighted with the moon behind it. The other two dudes come down and say, "fuck is that?" We stare at it. I finally walked up maybe 20 M from it, and it like hugs the tree. I can hear breathing, nothing. So, I walk away, and we call on the radio. So, they sent a Raven to take a peek at whatever we called up. Bear was a big thing, like stop training kind of animal. Similar to the horses on Polk. Command radios back that they we see it, and it has a mild heat signature. So I was like well maybe it's a plastic bag.

We just had a tornado slam through here a few weeks ago and trashed the training areas. So, we start to head out, and I look back at this tree and see that fucker jump down and crash, and we took off running. The Raven/BDE TOC said it looked like a giant cat. Fort Benning was saying maybe a Panther wandered up from Florida.

0333

This was about 5 almost 6 years ago.

I must also note that I was living in IHG Army Hotel Housing because I was attending a 5-month long school for the Army. The way the rooms were set up: I had a roommate and we share a "room". I had my own bedroom but I shared a kitchen and bathroom with my roommate and he has his own bedroom. The walls of our respective bedrooms' backup to each other and the walls were super thin. I could hear everything he did and he could hear everything I did in my room. I also need to mention that he was a very light sleeper. If I even rolled over in bed and one of the springs in my bed made a squeak, he would wake up (I know this because he would sigh loudly as to let me know that I woke him up at which point I say "sorry" out loud and we both go back to sleep).

This started out as any regular Thursday. My alarm went off at 4:00am and I was up and moving. I went about my usual daily activities and I finally got home that Thursday night at around 6:30pm. Because every day of the week was like this, by the time I got home I was extremely tired. I finished any work that might need to be done, I took a shower and then I got in bed. I got in bed at about 10pm. I fell asleep shortly after and drifted off to dreamland. (*Usually, I never have dreams. I just fall asleep and wake up without any recollection of where my mind goes while I am asleep*) This night was different. Very different. My dream starts off with me laying in bed and my eyes are closed. I can hear the quiet buzz of the light in the hallway just outside my room and the sound of the heating system winding and blowing air softly. All of the sudden, I hear the giggle of a little girl and open my eyes. I am not alarmed; I am just curious. I see every detail of my room in my dream.

My phone is plugged-in to the right of me on the bedside table. I see the blinding big blue numbers of my alarm clock sitting across the room below my tv. The time reads 3:33am. I see my desk, my laptop lying on it and next to it a bottle full of dip spit. This is so real to me. I am lost in all the detail of this dream... Then I realize it. I cannot move. My body is frozen with paralysis. I hear the giggle of the girl again. Now I am beginning to worry. There are no families with children in this building, only single Soldiers. Even if this is a dream, I know that for a fact. As I am looking down at my feet trying to get even the slightest wiggle from my toes, something, anything that would make me move and break this spell I notice something. Something is wrong.

There is someone standing in my room. Something I should say. It isn't standing on the ground. It's just hovering. I make out the silhouette of a person. This dark black outline of a man is standing in front of me. Had I not been frozen with paralysis; I would have jumped at this realization. I am struck with confusion for not knowing who this uninvited guest is, standing before me but I fear no one (or so I thought). I look further up to make eye contact with this person, this thing that was standing in my bedroom at 0300 in the morning. I want to look this thing in the eyes and let it know that as soon as I can move, it will be leaving my bedroom. As my eyes move higher and higher, the first thing I noticed was the smile.

This fucking smile. It was the creepiest smile I have ever seen in my life. The only way I could describe it is when someone smiles too hard, an almost extreme exaggeration. Its head was tilted sideways but something else was off. I could see no cheekbones. The nose and eyes were also missing. All I could see was that fucking creepy ass smile. Just smiling at me. A smile that let me know that it knew I was unable to move. This is where fear set in.

I try to sit up. I am fighting with all my might to jolt myself out of this paralysis. I just need to wake up from this dream. It's just a dream but I cannot move. At this point all I can think to do is scream. Maybe this will wake me. Nothing. Nothing comes out of my mouth. Panicking I try again... I manage to whisper to myself "GET UP". Then... an explosion or what sounds like an explosion goes off in my head. BOOM!!!

I wake up from my dream, confused as hell looking around my room. Everything is in order. My phone is plugged-in to the right of me on the bedside table. I see the blinding big blue numbers of my alarm clock sitting across the room below my tv. The time reads 3:33am. I see my desk, my laptop lying on it and next to it a bottle full of dip spit. Wait.. the time reads 3:33am.. I am awake. How does the time now and the time in my dream line-up exactly? As I stare at the clock, I notice a slight movement to the left of the clock. That fucking smile! A cold chill races down my spine. I feel my body lock into place. I am once again paralyzed. This thing advances toward me. I am completely terrified at this point.

I still cannot move. I know my pocket knife is in the drawer next to my bed. If I can grab it then everything will be just fine. I tell my mind to move my arm. Nothing. WHY CAN'T I FUCKING MOVE?!?!? It is getting closer and closer. It moves incredibly slow almost like it knows that it can take its precious time. I am not going anywhere. I am at the mercy of this creature. Once again, all I can thing to do is yell. Nothing. Nothing comes out of my mouth. My only chance was to wake up my roommate and hopefully he senses the panic in my voice. I cannot even squeak out a whisper. I know I am doomed now. I take a deep breath and I close my eyes, accepting the fact that I have no control over this situation. As I am laying there, frozen still with my eyes tightly closed, I hear the giggle of a little girl.

The same giggle that I heard in my dream. Without even wanting to, almost as a reflex that I cannot control, I open my eyes. This thing is literally a foot away from me. It is now hovering vertically over me and my bed. That fucking smile. I am in complete and utter desperation now. My eyes are shut as tightly as they can be. I just want this to end. Whatever it was planning to do, I just wanted it to happen. By some miracle, I am released from my state of paralysis and my body shoots up with my fist heading for where this thing is fucking smiling at me. As I am swinging upward, my eyes open and I see nothing. Nothing at all. My room is empty of any life besides my own.

Then I hear it again. The giggle of this little girl is outside of my room. The door to my bedroom is shaking. (HOW THE FUCK IS MY ROOMMATE STILL ASLEEP) As the giggling stops, I hear the whimpering of a crying baby. The sound is getting further and further away though. It sounds as though it has left our "room" and is traveling away, down the hall. Everything is dead silent except the quiet buzz of the light in the hallway just outside my room and the sound of the heating system winding and blowing air softly. Still have no idea what happened. Didn't go back to sleep that night. Roommate thought it was hilarious when I told him.

NTC Creature

Okay, so I didn't start believing in any of this shit until I went to NTC in 2016 and had an experience with a Wendigo/Skinwalker, coincidentally enough in 2016 at NTC. Never saw it though, only heard, smelled, and felt it. For a long time, it was just something I would think about or thought I dreamed until I talked to this full-blooded Navajo dude when I got out, and he said it was a Skinwalker or Wendigo.

To preface the experience, I spent most of my childhood in nature, hunting, fucking off stalking animals, and became significantly in tune with nature. I can feel the changes in the earth as beings move through it, and definitely if they were looking at me. Fast forward to Fort fucking Irwin in 2016, I find myself as a lonely observer on a mountain top observing a pass after 3/4 of our battalion was killed and our fearless leaders FASCAM'd what was left of the unit into a valley.

I was on my OP by myself with two Strykers worth of Soldiers at the mountain base. I would walk down for resupply, but I was by my lonesome with an LLDR for three days and nights. The last night I was up there just doing my thing, probably 0300 in the morning, and I started feeling there was something near me. At first, I assumed a giant jackrabbit was moving somewhere around me and brushed it off.

About 15 minutes later and the feeling is back. It feels like something bigger is nearby. Assume it's a mountain goat or one of the donkeys' people keep talking about, and shortly after that, I can hear something moving around (probably 200 yards away, dead of night). It begins to move closer, and the feeling of indifference and curiosity turns into fear. I begin to notice the sounds moving closer.

I knew it was not a hooved animal simply from its steps, and the cadence that it was moving made me think it was a biped for sure, and I started wondering what the fuck it could be. I pop on my PSQ-20 and pick up nothing on NVG or thermal on the mountain. Just the vehicles, sleep area, and two Soldiers on guard a bit away. I decided to stop observing and face how I could hear this thing, all while I began to feel what I can only describe as dread. Dread so pure I can feel it in my teeth. I had nothing but blanks, so I grabbed my hunting knife and kept it on me.

I heard the creature move toward me in a zig-zag pattern ever so slowly, pausing to listen or smell and then advancing towards me. Around the time I felt that scary feeling was when I noticed a stench of rotting flesh getting worse until my eyes almost burned from it. I was frozen in some odd state for probably five minutes until I felt the presence recede away from me. That was it.

I didn't say a fucking thing to another until I discovered this page and saw other people having accounts like the feeling of fear and the rotting smell, which was all just affirmation to me I wasn't crazy. But, as I said before, I never saw the thing. I didn't go to sleep that night, and once the sun started to come up I went and tried to find some tracks (which I swear to God, I can track a thing or two).

There was NOTHING on the ground for tracks. The only tracks I could find were on vegetation, but it's more challenging to catch a line on an animal that way, and it was too sporadic to track or assume it was all from the same animal.

It fucked with me, man. The noises of it moving would almost change as it progressed. Like I said, never anything hooved, that's very distinct, but it was like a big cat taking its time stalking something, but almost like its feet were changing. From paws to claws to bare feet or something. Unless there were three fuckin things taking turns fucking with me. But I knew it could see me and was moving towards me. I could feel both of its eyes on me like someone was pushing two fingers against the base of my neck. It was like I was hanging out in a barren wasteland. Like a tiger or some other apex predator teleported next to me out of the blue. Fucking crazy.

I can say with almost certainty it was not a cougar. The way it moved couldn't have been feline, especially with how far away I heard it. If it were a cougar after me, I wouldn't be here. Also, large cats are incredibly elusive. They would have been way out of their area upon our arrival with Strykers running and that many people around. They have a massive range and would have happily fucked off. Also, if it were just an animal, my body wouldn't have responded like that. I can't even describe the gripping fear. I never let anything like it before that, and not since. There was no fight or flight. It was like I went into the brain stem and froze. I feel like a bitch for acting the way I did. Being the outdoorsman, I think I am. It was just different. I could feel dread in my teeth. That's how I can describe it like bone-chilling dread.

Dogman In The Back 40

I'm stationed at Fort Campbell, Kentucky. The training area we have is called the "Back 40." Thousands of acres of ranges and training sites. My story takes place in the Back 40 near a make shift town called "Cassidy". It's located in the middle of nowhere surrounded by forest and thick underbrush and at that time it was mid-July so everything was in full bloom. My company was conducting a two-week field problem in this area and after we had secured this town my platoon was tasked with pulling a blocking position about 100 meters into the wood line from this town.

So, this is like day 12 of the two-week field problem I'm located on the far-right area of our blocking position with my squad. I'm a squad leader of my infantry platoon and we dig into our position. I'm located 10-15 meters from my Soldiers with my back up against a tree. Darkness sets on the Back 40, the guys are tired, and my team leaders are doing their checks to ensure the guys are awake. Hours go by and I didn't keep track of time but if I had to guess it was around midnight. No moon. Only thing you could see was to our rear where the town of Cassidy was located. My alpha team leader is laying with his team on the line and we're pulling a 50/50 security detail so one man up the other asleep. My bravo team leader is sleeping next to me. Our platoon Radio man (RTO) was walking back and forth behind us bouncing between my squad and the others all on line in this blocking position.

So, every 20-30 minutes I hear him walking by and eventually he comes to me and says "Hey sergeant you good on radio batteries?" "I'm good dude," I reply. So being used to hearing him walking by so much, I hear something, and not even thinking about it I ignore it. Then it gets closer and closer and a lot slower in movement.

I look over my shoulder and say "what the fuck are you doing" and that's when I saw whatever it was in a mid-crouch pose about 20 meters from me making low subtle growling noises like a dog or wolf. I froze and felt the hair on the back of my neck stand and my heart start to race. Whatever this was stood at least 5 foot tall crouched over sinking lower and lower to the ground. Paralyzed with confusion and fear I watch for another 10-12 seconds. I then reach and grabbed my e-tool, not taking my eyes off what I'm looking at. Then quickly flip my PSQ-20s (night vision) and as I did this the creature ran in a diagonal line from me fast (and when I say fast booking it in a low stance). I flip my 20s to thermal and I saw the outline of this thing running.

Everyone around me heard it crashing through the woods. It ran too fast to be a man and too big to be a deer as it was fully standing up as it crashed through the brush.

Later that night another squad leader told me he heard loud deep sniffing noises near his position. His Soldiers were saying they smelled what appeared to resemble a wet dog smell. In the hours before dawn we all heard this loud-guttural noise that would start up immediately after the coyotes. Coyotes are prominent in the area and you always hear them. Except after this howl or loud noise they all instantly stopped. I had always heard stories and never believed it as well as others in my platoon. After this encounter we all agreed we were not alone that night and something lurks out there.

It was canine by the look of it, it was dark I don't want to speculate and give a false tale but in the face it was elongated like a snout from what I could see. I grew up playing in the woods, camping and hunting I'd never have seen heard or felt that way ever

Fort Bragg Bricks

So, on Fort Bragg, the barracks are pretty dated. Especially the 1st BCTs Infantry footprint. Probably three to four times a year, someone dies on the footprint, and no one seems to have any explanation of why. From people literally diving off the balcony to taking a ton of muscle relaxers and fading away.

Anyway, over the course of four years living on this footprint, many other dudes and I have shared experiences of entities and energies radiating from various rooms. One night I was getting ready to bed down. It was a long weekend, and we stayed up until about two to three partying, so it was late. Laying down about to fade off sleep, I hear my closet door close, scares the shit out of me, and snap me awake.

I investigate, and as I'm walking to the door, the light turns on inside, and I hear a slight thud and something putting weight above the ceiling. I didn't even open the door. I went over to my buddy's room. We met in the hallway because he heard the same thing coming from his closet.

We never figured out what it was, but I had so much shit in my closet there's no way anything could've been in there making noise. We gave the entity a name and began living amongst it as if we accepted its presence, and it wouldn't bother us anymore.

We would all feel very dark and evil vibes from those walls. I've heard of dudes seeing Soldiers in their rooms, dude's doors getting knocked on by no one, regular spooky shit.

Leschi Town

Leschi town (MOUT site at JBLM, WA). As OPFOR, our platoon stayed in the most western building next to the HLZ. One night, I heard someone knocking hard as fuck on the door in the room I was in.

I opened it, and no one was at the door. Then I heard the sound of footsteps running up and down the stairwell. I asked who was there, but no one answered. I shined my headlamp with the white light on down the stairs, nobody was down there, but I could still hear the footsteps of someone running up. Yet I could see nobody down the stairs.

I immediately thought someone was either fucking with me (which I asked the dudes, and everyone said they were all knocked out that night except for the guys pulling guard outside), or I was just tired as fuck. I pretty much said fuck it and went back to sleep.

The UXO Call

So when we arrived and the TL was moving between the response truck and UXO, I was looking around (the first time being up in that post area). Saw in the tree line what I thought was someone walking. Allegedly people like to go up that way to gather mushrooms?

Anyways, I'm about to call out to the person as they pass between trees that they can't be there, it's an active EOD incident and a possible explosive hazard. They just vanish. I told my TL when he returned, and we walked over to find them for safety reasons. I couldn't find a trace of them.

The thing that makes it even weirder was that the person was dressed in 1850s uniform garb with a satchel (the part that made me think of mushroom gathering). The only time I saw what I believe to be a ghost. I guess Fort Riley has some spooky features to it, like Camp Funston and WW1 Soldiers from the Spanish flu or the Calvary Parade field.

Fort Bragg Witch

Honestly surprised I hadn't seen it on here yet. There's a church in the middle of the training area out of Bragg that's abandoned as far as I can tell. Creepy old civil war mass graves and one graveyard actually at the church with headstones. I had heard stories about it and didn't think much of it, but there's this weird feeling I get whenever I'm around it.

Even sat in a patrol base pretty close to it, but as freaked out as we were, nothing too crazy was seen. But another time I was coming back from a deer hunt a few weeks later, and I saw dark figure with piercing white eyes. That's my whole experience.

Research of the area dates back from the Salem witch trials, mass graves to civil war, exorcism in the '70s, the Wiccan movement of the early 2000s.

Felt like a witch, in all honesty. I know I'm not the only one who's seen it in or around the church. Most others don't say anything about the eyes, just a tiny womanly figure. People see shadows in the windows and feelings of being watched. People would catch glimpses of things on the inside the past windows.

NTC OPFOR

I'm OPFOR, and last rotation, we had an SBCT from JBLM come as RTU, and we had dropped off camo nets for an infantry platoon from JBLM. They were guest OPFOR near our hide site about 500 meters north of us in these old buildings.

So fast forward about eight hours later, it was about 0300, my TC and I just got done pulling our guard shift. I was putting my cot together on the back deck of my OSV, and I started to hear footsteps near us. I whispered to my TC asking if he heard it, and he did too, so he grabbed our NVGs. We're looking all around us and don't see shit. This goes on for about 15 minutes, then stops. So, I bed down and about 10 minutes later I hear them again but close as shit, and I'm yelling out, "Hey, who is there," and hear the footsteps.

I'm still looking around through my NVGs and still can't see shit. It was too loud of footsteps to be a coyote too. You could hear them get closer and closer. Then they stopped, then when they started back up again it was louder footsteps, and it sounded liked they were circling us.

But then it stops again, and we wake up the following day. I'm so exhausted I got about 2 hours of sleep, and our LMTV drops our chow off to us for our whole platoon and our guest OPFOR attachment. So, we drive around dropping off chow to everyone at their hide sites, and we go up to the GBH. I asked a couple of them if they had anybody go down to us last night around 0300, and they said no. They were the only ones anywhere near us. So, no idea what it could have been.

The Runner

I was on Fort Stewart, probably summer of 2016. My platoon was out in the middle of nowhere. We were practicing route reconnaissance. At the time, I was a lowly PFC and the driver of our truck. We were told to expect OPFOR, but I guess it didn't happen how we were expecting.

As a truck crew, we had been awake about 36 hours. Our unit was mindlessly firing ammo into the woods so that they could get the same amount next year. You know how it is. So anyway, the CO was feeling fun and called out trucks to spin up.

We did. Then we went on a patrol. After a couple of hours, I started seeing a guy in my NVGs. He was sprinting at my truck. I'd call him to the gunner, he'd check with his thermals on the 240, but he didn't see shit. It happened three times that night. I was too tired to care, but nowadays I think about what I saw, it scares me. I remember his eyes. He was mad.

The other truck called contact right shortly after I saw him. I don't know if he was doing his thing or if we saw the same thing. He was in a uniform, like what you'd wear on the field. But he wasn't kitted up or anything like. He scared the shit out of me. Like I said, 36 hours without sleep. But boy, I DONT KNOW how you can come up with that angry motherfucker running at my truck in your mind

The Lurking Soldier

I'll preface this with some background. Both these stories happened at Drum during the summer/early autumn of 2020. It was during a CALFEX we were doing. It was like 0200- "ish", and I got woken up for radio guard.

I got out of my "fart sack" [i.e. sleeping bag], and I'm walking over to grab the radio when I see a dude wearing a fleece jacket with a red lens on looking down at a book and mumbling something to himself. When I walked by, he locked eyes with me but didn't say anything. He just stood there on the edge of our patrol base.

Later that night, I heard screaming in the woods during my shift. So I asked some dudes in my platoon the following day if they saw or heard anything and a few other dudes confirmed what I saw. They even heard the screaming. Saw the same dude in a fleece jacket and red lens-standing at the edge of the patrol base, just lurking.

I'd always heard Skinwalkers had to be invited in your home to be able to enter, so I had a dumbass theory that maybe I saw a Skinwalker. Still, he couldn't do anything because he hadn't been invited into the patrol base, it sounds stupid, but it was an idea I had.

The other story takes place a few weeks earlier during PLT STX. This one may have been a hallucination, but since two guys saw the same thing, I'm not sure. At that point, we'd been going on close to 30 hours with no sleep and were crossing an LDA about 75 or so meters up the road from a bridge.

One of our 240 gunners told me he saw Soldiers in kit appear, walk up to the bridge, jump into the water and drown. He looked over at the guy next to him, and he'd seen the same thing too. Usually, I'd think they saw shit, but it's weird they had the same hallucination

A Simpler Story

Well, this one is a little simpler. We had gone out to the ranges right outside of Lewis to get ready for EFMB coming up, so they had us doing a lot of land navigation and vehicle land navigation while we were out there. I got lucky, and one of the Joe's NVGs batteries died.

So I lent them my NVGs and slept in the back of the vehicle while they did land navigation. At the end of the night, at like 0100, we set up a sleeping spot. The females got the vehicles and the males got too rough it in their bivies outside. Since I had been sleeping during training, I couldn't rack out relatively as quickly as everyone else. I sat there talking to the fireguard and ended up heading to the wood line to piss.

Well, hitting the wood line, I heard a lot of movement out in the woods, which I had just assumed was animals and shit. I came back to my sleeping and decided to pull my PT cap down and get some sleep. I heard a bloodcurdling scream what felt like pretty close to our spot.

I sat up and looked at the fireguard, who was staring off into the same area as me. We both heard it and agreed that it wasn't a deer. We decided to wake up our NCO, who told us we were retarded, and to relax. I laid down after that and got a terrible sleep until my fireguard shift. Then every single thing I caught in my headlamp felt like it was moving.

NTC Skinwalker

I went to NTC around 2016, which, as everyone knows, is in the middle of the desert in California. We had just arrived a couple of days prior and grabbed our vehicles from the railhead. So now we have a sandy motor pool full of Strykers. I was with the medics and we decided we needed a guard on our MEVs overnight.

So being with one of the infantry platoons, I pulled the second night of guard duty for four hours with our recon medic. We got out to the vehicles around 2300 and had a four-hour watch until we got relief. I remember bullshitting with the other record for about an hour until he had told me he had never dipped before. So being the Soldier I was, I had to convince him to try some Copenhagen.

He sat there for about five minutes before he looked at me a little loopy and said he had to take a crap. While he walked away, I just stared off into space. This motor pool section of RUBA had streetlights lighting the vehicles throughout.

During my thoughts, I finally saw some movement that caught my eye. I turned my head and looked in the direction of the vehicles, and I saw a perfectly illuminated and hairless doglike creature hunched over on two legs under the light. Like hunched over like raptor from Jurassic Park. Its front "paws" were pulled in like a dog laying down

Staring at me, and its eyes were shining like a dog that a flash flight had just hit. We stared down for the longest seconds of my life, and then it turned and dipped away.

It had looked like I caught it in headlights when I looked at it, and it had frozen staring directly at me. It made a noise skittering along, kind of like a rat when I saw it move into my vision space. I saw it lean onto its front paws. That's when I took a double-take, and it was gone

I shook myself. When my partner came back from the porta shitter, I told him, and he said it was probably a coyote with mange. But every time I think about it, I can't help but wonder why a mangey coyote would be on its hind legs looking directly at me.

I had two NCOs and a couple of other medics tell me they saw the same thing waking around the vehicles around midnight every night until we started movement.

Fort Huachuca Part I

There were two times I saw a UFO: once during the day and two times at night.

If anyone has ever been to Fort Huachuca, they all know the long PT road that takes them to the airport gate, and then mountain base. This road is pretty long, and many battalions do their fair share of running, rucking, and PT tests. One morning we had been doing a buddy run, and we were running down the road towards the airport.

My team leader and I usually had a similar pace, so we would always run together. We had seen this black disk come down from the cloud's way out over the far mountain range towards Tucson. This thing has to be making time because of how quickly it got from one side of the range to the other in a matter of seconds. As soon as it had started moving over the mountains, we had heard the F-22's startup and begin to take off. It was pretty good coincidence that these guys were taking off as this thing was moving away. I think they were chasing it/responding to it.

This other range is around 90-120 miles away from where we are in Sierra Vista. Anyways, by the time these pilots had responded to it, it was already moving back up into the atmosphere. It had all happened within 2-3 minutes.

The second time was when we were in closeout formation, waiting for our CSM to start talking. I had been looking up (just memorizing the clouds as any bored SPC would do) and I had happened to notice a silver disk that was moving in weird angles to match the outline of the clouds. I had pointed it out to another guy next to me, and we both watch it until the other clouds had moved in below it blocking our view, never being seen again.

Fort Huachuca Part II

The first time we had seen the lights at night was when we would sit in the back of my truck, drinking, and talking while watching lightning storms over Tucson in the distance. The stars were bright, but we had been out there almost every night to the point we knew if something was different.

This night we were talking as usual (not drinking) and we had seen these green and orange flashing lights moving fast before the coming to a stop. So, we looked up what airplane lights look like on their wings, and it wasn't matching up to anything.

These lights would hover in an area outside of the storm for another 15 minutes before shooting up and out of sight within the blink of an eye. All we saw was the stream of light that something makes when it moves stupid fast really quick. We all agreed that it was weird and continued with our conversation.

Fort Huachuca Part III

The last experience that I had with the lights would be when I was out in the field shooting comms. We ran 24/7 comm switching parameters with NETOPS to make sure everything was fully functional. We had seen another light this time come down in a circular motion from over the border, over US airspace.

It wasn't too far away from us, but we were watching it with big eyes. It was just hovering near the blimp for a few minutes. It wasn't flashing colors like the last one we saw. This time it was just a blue light but brighter than anything I've ever seen. At the same time it had come down: we had lost signal and radio communications, so we couldn't even call it into the other team who had been closer to it on the other side of the valley. This time instead of beaming back up into the sky, it just disappeared in the blink of an eye.

Once it vanished, the signal came back. We had received a call from the officer on duty at the time, but we didn't know if we had a believable story… so we blamed it on a power issue. Four of us saw it and tried to get video proof, but nothing could be made out except the audio. We all just passed it off as another weird thing about Arizona without ever speaking of it again.

The Air Force has done a lot of exciting stuff out there, but do you know about the one airline that only goes to Area 51? We had this thing land there one time at our tiny runway. We had never had anything more significant than A10s land there before, so when I saw the commercial flight, it was bizarre.

OVERSEAS

Guantanamo Bay

I was mobilized there in September of 2020. I walked into one of the detention facilities that may or may not have been empty. My buddies who entered always got a bad vibe from that place. I was in there by myself. I was looking for a machine that was on our books when I heard footsteps above me.

Like I knew I was in there alone, so I got spooked. Then I heard voices and a door slam shut. The crazy part is that in the location it came from, all the doors were still open. It got frigid, like unnaturally cold for anywhere on the island. I "noped" the fuck out.

My buddy had the same experience with the voices. She was in there with one of our NCOs and heard voices behind her. Confused, she looked behind her and saw nothing. She asked him if he said something, and he was like, no. What could it have been?

Echoes Of The Korean War

It was 2018 in South Korea at the Twin Bridges Training Site. There are old Korean War trenches everywhere. We were out running missions, and that night at our patrol base we set out anti-intrusion systems. It was late at night, and the guys on watch started to notice the anti-intrusion devices going off and could hear what sounded like a platoon-sized element marching through the woods towards our position.

They woke everyone up in preparation for a fight. We sent a call back to the TOC giving a report, and they responded that no other elements were in the area (friendly or OPFOR). At this time, the

54

sound got louder and louder as the platoon size element marching through the woods was approaching.

Through the NVGs, multiple guys could see what looked like figures approximately 25m from the fighting positions and appear to march by and continue. No one slept that night, and we were spooked the entire time we were out there training. No doubt those woods are haunted by the men who fought and died in the Korean War. On both sides.

Wheeler Army Airfield

My unit was based out of Hanger 4 at the time. As the night shift NCOIC for my section, there were numerous times, even during the summer, I would be out on the ramp and hit an area where the temperatures would feel like it dropped about 20 degrees or working on a bird in the hanger and feel something hard brushing against you.

I was always weirded out if I had to pass by Hanger 3 or go to the ramp area in the back of it. The wildest experience was when I was doing some office work for the CAP unit. I was the only person in the building, and entry was via a cipher lock. I heard the door open, and I called out that I was in an office.

The only light on was the entryway and where I was. I heard footsteps moving in an adjacent hallway, and I investigated who it was. I called out but got no answer, so I figured it was someone messing with me.

I grabbed a flashlight to shine down the hall and saw nothing but still heard the footsteps, and it sounded like they went into a closed office yet the door neither opened nor closed.

The footsteps came back out into the hall and went toward the front of the building where the entrance was. As I looked at the door, I heard it open and then shut, yet there was no physical movement of the door. I wrapped up what I was doing and left the building.

I told someone about the encounter, and they had a similar experience. Looking up the history of the building, it was hit by a bomb during the attack that damaged the front of the building. I was skeptical about the paranormal until that night, made me a believer.

Cambri Fritch Kaserne

US Army Vet. Just after the War in Iraq started in 2002. I ran a dining facility on Cambri Fritch Kaserne in Darmstadt Germany.

When the ground war started the MPs would call me every night saying my building was unsecure. After about a week of this I was tired of it, but nothing I did would stop it.

One night when I was clearing the building with the MP's the radio in the building was on, and they told me that they already cleared that building and there was no radio on. In fact, it was a strange night for them.

While in the building which sat on a hill, a dense fog rolled in, and they could see WWII Nazi Soldiers marching in the fog. They could hear them marching all around the building, but when they came out of the building there was nothing in the fog.

I could tell they were at their wits end and were totally freaked out. As soon as they announced the ground war ended, so did the open DFAC doors and marching German Soldiers.

"Huh, that's weird."

Hohenfels Training area in Germany 2018. We air assaulted into the DZ at like 0300 in the morning. About three hours later, just before twilight, I'm pulling security and two of the OC's come walking toward me, one in front and one about 5 meters behind him.

I couldn't tell who it was, just the outline of two guys walking toward me. I didn't have my NVGs on for crossover, so it was essentially just bodies walking at me until one of them identified himself.

When the first one got up to me, I asked him how they were doing and realized the other hadn't shown up.

So I asked him if he had another guy with him, and he said no. I got the chills immediately and told him another dude was walking behind him, to which he replied, "huh, that's weird."

Intruders In The Ahkio

I had what I can only describe as some paranormal experience out at DTA in Alaska. While out at squad live-fire, we were sleeping in the Ahkio's (10-man Arctic tent), and I awake to the strangest feeling of someone pushing and attempting to hold me down.

When I look up, there's some grayish/black shadowy figure who was kneeling beside me and looking down at me. When I realized what was happening, I had to fight to sit myself up, and as I look over, I see two more of those figures above two of the other guys in the tent.

After I made what I assume is eye contact with them, they disappeared. I didn't see them any of the other days, but that overall experience weirded me out.

I wish I had more to say about it. It wasn't sleeping paralysis because I've personally never experienced it, and unless it just comes out of the blue, I think it was something real. The strangest part was I could feel something on me like a person pushing and trying to hold me down.

Hohenfels

I have quite a few weird-ass anecdotes from Hohenfels. I was there 2014-2015, and when I first got there, the barracks were being renovated. On BN Staff Duty, the NCOIC checked those barracks because of flickering lights we could see from the BN HQ entrance.

Because it was being renovated, no one was supposed to be there. Long story short, a NCO kept chasing after lights flickering on and off but whatever he was chasing was stupid fast, like 1st floor to 3rd floor to the other stairwell back to 1st floor, etc. It was nothing super concrete but weird nonetheless.

Two homies from my PLT knock on my door at night, freaking out about their room and wanting to crash on my couch. Something grabbed their trashcan, pulled it all out, and spread it all around their room.

When they woke up, all they woke up to was trash everywhere. It could have been an animal or something, except they were on the third floor, which would have been a weird place.

We had one PVT (crazy dude, should have never been allowed into the Army) start spray painting pentagrams on the inside of his barracks room window. His roommate saw this and saw the dude cutting himself.

I ran downstairs to let CQ know. The dude was bonkers. The rumor was that the chaplain was asked to perform an exorcism on him. He got chaptered, I think. Unfortunately, he never got the help he needed and committed suicide.

The craziest finds were in the box. Box Witch stories aside, guys swear they found a cave with wrought iron bars set blocking the entrance. They were able to get someone in, and allegedly old boy found human bones, along with a skull that he kept hidden away once he took it. Pretty crazy. We all thought it was funny.

I came across some weird sort of "prayer circle" in the land nav area. It could have been a camp way back when, but the dismembered toy dolls left there were weird. I remember getting a chill when stumbling upon it and going quickly.

The boars in the land nav area chased guys all the time. We all hated night land nav. Red lens headlamps and empty M4s aren't a great defense against a spooked boar.

Tons of guys willingly failed land nav after getting chased by the pigs. I swear all of Hohenfels was out to out us. The boars were giant there, too.

A bunch of guys would always have sleep paralysis. Shadow people were sitting on their chest staring at them, figures looking around corners at guys while they slept.

Someone's door just clean fell off of their closet as if someone removed the hinges and unlocked the door. We always had those German maintenance guys fixing something. I guess the Nazi ghosts didn't like us.

In Hohenfels, we have the Box Witch, but that has the same name everywhere. Legend had it that during WW2, there were towns in the training area with Germans living in them.

As the Allies moved deeper and deeper into Germany, they were bombing villages and towns, including the ones in what is now the box. One of the towns had a little girl.

She got caught outside and never made it to a shelter before the firebombs got her. Decades later, Hohenfels got set up as a NATO training base. Allegedly, a Polish Soldier noted that he saw a little girl dressed in black during a training exercise.

He didn't think anything of it and stuck around, trying to talk to her. He disappeared, and a massive search went underway for him. They found him on the other side of the Box, dead and bloated within a day, a distance that he couldn't have possibly moved to on his foot power.

So as the warning goes, if you see the girl in white, you have to help her with whatever request she gives you. If you see her in black, stay far away and get out of there. At least that's what we got told.

I remember a National Guardsman that got augmented to us calling up that he saw a little girl in the box, but it was some severe scuttlebutt, and we are pretty sure someone put him up to it. Still, guys swear they had seen her before.

Camp Humphreys

So I was stationed at Camp Humphreys in Korea for a year. If you're unfamiliar, it's on a relatively rural part of the west coast, but it's Korea, so you're never really far from civilization. The base itself is divided by an airfield. Regular army on the south side, general/joint staffs, and spooks on the north, with only the latter living there.

59

I was shamming, getting ready to out the process, so I was working out late and sleeping in. Which is why I went out for a run one night at 0100 in the morning. I had hit my turnaround and was headed back and saw a bright light off to my right over the central residential part of base. Hung out for a few seconds, then started falling at an angle toward the horizon.

I didn't hear a sound when it appeared, which tripped me up at the time but looking at a map now, the Yellow Sea is about 50 miles away. So if it impacted there, it would have crossed the horizon but I digress.

I booked it back to my room, I didn't hear anything from the patriot battery along the way, so they didn't pick up whatever it was. I grabbed my badge, went into the office at 0200 still in my workout clothes, and checked the kinds of official sites where that sort of thing would get posted because I assumed someone got shot down and fight tonight would be real after 70 years.

Nothing. I called it a night, check back again the next day, and still nothing. Not sure how to end this, but it was September 21st last year if anyone else wrote it down and thought they were crazy too.

Stalhiem

2009 Benjamin Franklin Village in Mannheim, Germany. Our barracks were old Nazi barracks built-in 1939. Had swastikas on cornerstone handrails and few other places—one night lying in bed in the barracks trying to go to sleep. We were MPs, so we had troops coming and going constantly.

Around 0100, I heard footsteps marching up and down the hallway. Initially I thought it was CQ or someone going on or coming off shift, but it was pacing from one end then back. I got up to see what was going on.

I opened my door, and no one was there. It happened once every couple of months, and more and more people started hearing it. Eventually, people started talking about seeing a German Soldier with a black stahlhelm staring at them—multiple stories, but always the same description.

Fort Shafter

I'm a PFC at my first unit at Fort Shafter, Hawaii, on staff duty. The SDNCO had let me sleep on a cot for a while in a room about ten feet away and was now sleeping himself. The SD desk is situated at the at-intersection of two hallways, with a parallel hallway at the other end.

Makes the shape of an "H," with four doors at each corner. These three hallways service the entire first floor of the building, and you have a commanding view of the whole building from that desk. Behind me and to the right is a metal stairwell that goes up to the next floor. There is absolutely no way to access that stairwell without opening a loud side door and visible to the SD desk. Suddenly I hear footsteps clanging their way UP the stairs, which weirds me out. I go to check it out, and there's nothing there. I go up the stairs and the door that the stairwell accesses is locked. I go back down to the desk, and a little while later, I hear the footsteps coming back down. Naturally, no one came out of the stairwell.

This building had been around since the WWII era, and the field across the street is named after an SGT who unluckily caught a stray anti-aircraft round during the Pearl Harbor attack.

"Wer bist du? Was willst du?"

So I was in Graf for some 50-day gunnery supporting a CAB. It was free reign to do whatever the fuck we wanted. We were drinking, smoking, taking humvees to the commissary, making cooking fires, etc. The only people who came down to our part of town were range control, Romanian contractors, and Bundeswehr. Even when they showed up, they would take some MREs from our huge supply of them and fuck off. It was like paradise. I didn't do shit but KP and security.

So it's late at night, December, cold and rainy. I'm sitting outside pulling security because it's a "deployment." My team leader left for to get some chow, and I started a small warming fire with a bit of survival kit the wife got me. I'm sitting there drinking a few beers, smoking some cigs, watching the fire, and thinking of home when suddenly I look up, and there's a seven- or 8-foot-tall shadow man

61

in front of me.

It wasn't opaque. It made no noise, didn't move closer, just a shadow shaped like a man's silhouette. This dude was TALL as fuck. The shadow didn't make sense because the fire wasn't casting it. It was like it just existed. The way he was standing, his legs were shoulder-width apart, arms slightly outward like in a power stance, not exactly T posing or anything, but like he was ready to fight.

My heart was racing, and I felt choked up like I couldn't say anything; I started to look around me to see if he was casting a shadow. I finally started asking in English, "Hey, what's up, man?" Then in German, is ask "Wer bist du? Was willst du?" In case it's some German Soldier or contractor prowling about. Nothing.

It just stood there. I'm a little freaked the fuck out at this point because I have an unloaded M4 and a knife, and this shadow is just standing there, shuffling its weight from one foot to the other here and there. My heart was pounding, I heard a branch snap behind me. Without a single fucking sound, the shadow man just sprinted away, like he did not weigh a thing. I turned around to see what snapped a branch, and it was my team leader coming back with a couple of MREs. I was fucking terrified, and I didn't say anything. I just lit another cig and ate my pizza MRE.

We all heard and saw strange shit in the woods at night. Nobody else saw the shadow man that I saw. It was legitimately one of the most terrifying things that happened to me. It was one of the ranges at the Graf training area with those old tin shacks fenced in with wooden guard towers around it.

I'll never forget the cold chill I felt even though I was directly next to my warming fire. My heart was cold. All it did was just stand there and watch but every single fiber of my being felt threatened. Like almost a primal kind of fear. Like when our distant paleolithic ancestors huddled around fires in caves to keep safe.

Sometimes when I walk my dog at night I think about it again, I get that same sense of unease, then I tell my dog to hurry the fuck up so I can go back inside.

Soto Cano Air Base

Alright, so no shit there I was, Honduras 2017, doing the whole hearts and minds thing, which occurred during one of my nights on fireguard at the clinic. I and the senior medic are shooting the shit at the front desk just trying to stay awake as it's roughly around 0300ish and no patients have come in all night. So I decide to step outside to get some fresh air.

I'm standing there looking up in the sky and notice this bright ass light just hovering in one place. Mind you, I'm tired as shit, but I know this wasn't any ordinary light because the moon and stars were visible, and this wasn't our aircraft since the flight line wasn't running any night ops, so I'm scratching my head like what the fuck is that just hovering there?

It was a solid 10mins or so. I'm like, alright, I'm going to grab the medic and see what he thinks. As I step back to go towards the front doors, it flies in the quickest Z pattern I've ever seen then vanishes into thin air!

I'm talking fast, like when you write a big ass Z on a piece of paper with a marker. I was like, what the fuck just happened? So I run back in to grab the medic, and we come back out in case it reappeared, but it was long gone. I told him what happened, and he was like, either you're half asleep, or you just saw a UFO.

From that moment on, I was always on the lookout for the rest of the deployment but never saw it again. Some extraterrestrials pulling surveillance on us, and only a matter of time before we all start seeing their aircraft.

The Old Magic

I haven't seen anything, but my buddy and I were in Hohenfels for Swift Response in 2016 and had a weird experience. It was the night where the "big fight" was supposed to kick off. We were pulled to establish security in a wood line next to a large open field that I think was an LZ.

Well, we had been sitting there for probably three hours, bored as shit, but we heard lots of movement and snorts/snarls in the bushes behind us. My bud was behind me, trying to scope it out while I'm looking for movement on the LZ.

At first, we thought it was the following line of Soldiers acting as security, but we realized they would have moved up another 75 meters to be in that spot. The next (worse) thought, is we have a wild boar on our hands and we are both going to get gored to death with our only weapons having a shitty little BFA on it.

We sat there for easily another hour with this rustling and sound happening the entire time. Under NVGs, my bud can't see anything in this area like 20 meters away. Which is what he has been looking at this whole time—no movement, no identifiable shape, just snarls, and bushes moving. Then our MSG just comes walking straight through that bush like nothing and asks us for an update. As he walked through the bush the sounds and movement stop immediately. Nothing ran off or anything.

My bud is just still looking at that bush as I give him the generic "NSTR." He leaves and moves to the next LGOP. The LGOP pulling security like 75m behind us heard it too and thought it was us first. They also zoned in on the area of the bushes and never saw anything either. Just a weird and genuinely worrying experience.

I reminded my buddy of this recently, and all he says is, "Germany is full of all that old magic."

The White Shadow

We were at the beach fishing. It was dark as fuck, and the only light was the one from my buddy's headlamp. It was hot and humid the whole night. I was about 25-30 meters away from my buddies when out of nowhere, I saw this white mass/thing fly past me and go up the steps that lead to the beach.

I saw it, and it disappeared like halfway up. There was no way it could have been either of my buddies because one jumped in the ocean after his rod, and the other was standing there. It got unnaturally cold, and my arms were full of goosebumps. For the rest of the night, I felt like we were being watched.

GITMO is haunted as fuck. There were battles fought in Cuba during the OG Roosevelt presidency, and service members have died on the island before we ever got there. Plus the whole history of the base in recent years. There's a really bad vibe all around.

Conn Barracks Schweinfurt

I did not witness or anything, but it was common knowledge on our base that a specific barracks room was never assigned after the third Soldier had committed suicide in it. Friends in barracks management later confirmed that it was condemned for this reason.

A lot of people had sleep paralysis in said building. Many of us had the same recurring dream, Including me.

In the dream, we would wake up strapped to a gurney in an operating room. Doctors would then come into the room and begin to conduct experiments on you in the dream. Freaky, like something out of a horror movie. But multiple people in these barracks had the same recurring dream, details always the same. It is essential to know that this base was formally a mental hospital for German Soldiers after WWII.

NATIONAL GUARD AND RESERVES

Pohakuloa Training Area

It's not just a personal experience but from others in the Hawaii Guard, 25th ID, and Marines that probably experienced it up on Pohakuloa Training Area (PTA). Pretty much PTA sits on an elevation between Mauna Loa and Mauna Kea, the two most prominent mountains in the whole state of Hawaii. If you have been there, you would know for yourself, cold throughout the day with rolling fog or rain that lowers your visibility more and more. PTA is also a place stuck in time itself. Besides all the lava fields dried up over thousands of years, you can't help but feel like you're in another world sometimes. It's a sacred place in Hawaiian culture and holds a special place in our history. I am Native Hawaiian myself and grew up very superstitious about certain things, especially when it comes to culture.

Recently we went up there [PTA] for a range qual, the first in a long time since before COVID (since most of us have been on orders for the response). We bedded down at this little ravine area overlooking the zero range near this shoot house. I fall sound asleep and wake up around 0300 in my tent feeling very dizzy and lost in a sense. Felt like somebody was walking around, but I forced myself to sleep, paying no mind to it. The following day, I mention it, and one of the NCOs in the tent woke up at the same time to chanting and something moving towards him around 0300. "No doubt, Night Marchers," he said. Night Marchers or "Huaka'I Po" in Hawaiian, are the literal spirits of deceased warriors from ancient Hawaii. They move on the old grounds and trails even in death to protect the land. Dudes have felt, seen, and heard most of these while at PTA. One of the guys I was with reported seeing a steady stream of fire-like torches moving up a hillside, but nothing was visible through the

NVGs. I have heard from others that have been pushed at night and also heard the chanting. Best not to mess with the Night Marchers.

The best story I have was from a Staff Sergeant in the Hawaii National Guard. He said while they were doing a movement into one side of PTA, he heard what sounded like drums in the distance. I was the RTO (or radio operator), and he radioed in and asked, "you guys making noises on your movement?" I was told to tell him, "Negative we are maintaining deliberate and stealthy movement to the objective." So, imagine our surprise when we see the torches pass 60-70 meters away from us, and everyone began to hear the chanting. Headquarters was to our rear a few hundred meters away; they woke up the next morning to rock stacks (a sign of a sacred area in Hawaiian culture) on the hoods of the Humvees and decided to jump to a new location the same day.

I have seen them and felt them since, and they still scare me when I go out to PTA. To those who train at PTA: mind your movement and know your walking in a place that doesn't belong to you.

Fort Pickett

This was 2019 during our annual summer training. We were in the field, which is basically like camping in tents. There was a large open field where the medical tent was, and then our tents were back in the tree-line. There were a few nights where people were woken up by something shaking their tents, whispering their names or vivid nightmares. Some even saw figures standing outside their tents. Some people had dreams of waking up only to be in another dream.

I was with another sergeant in a two-person tent far off to the edge of the group. One night, I heard footsteps around our tent, almost circling it. As if a whole platoon was walking past us... slowly. But our medical area was so far away from all of the other training areas, and as far as I knew, no one was out training at 0200 that day.

(Not paranormal, but the whole place was INFESTED with spiders. When we first got there, we went into the woods to set up our sleeping tents. Within five minutes, six spiders were crawling on my pant legs. Not my favorite annual training)

OP Empire Shield

The New York Army National Guard had Operation Empire Shield going on after 9/11. Late January or early February of 2005 I was at Ginna Nuke Plant in Ontario, NY. I was on the 2nd shift, and it was wintertime because the weather was cold; it was dark early, but I don't remember much snow being on the ground.

One ne SGT and I were in an M998 hummer and just chilling after we had chow. So, sitting in the two-seater, we were talking about paranormal stuff. He was from Mexico and filling me in on what they believed on how people can be cursed and have them removed, Sanitaria and their local superstitions and all that.

So as we're sitting there around 2100, the empty back part of the Humvee has this LOUD slap or what I described as an extremely large toolbox being dropped in the ass-end of Rover East as we called it.

The SGT and I looked at each other, then out the vinyl window behind us. Then we busted out of the vinyl doors and started looking around like WHAT THE FUCK JUST HAPPENED!?!?! Whatever "IT" was, it was able to either slap or land in the bed of the M998 and drop the ass end of it down a good 10 to 12 inches at least. We wore simple IBAs for small arms protection, Army Combat Helmets (ACH), and we had M16A2s with a mag loaded and one in our ammo pouch.

We got out, looked around the parking lot we were in, and saw NOTHING. We were posted upright in the middle of this lot. The tree line, which always gave me a feeling of being watched by a few sets of eyes, was quickly 50 to 60 yards to our east. We had an admin building behind us to the north by about another 35 to 50 yards away.

I got up on the roll bar weighing 220 at the time and tried to mimic the impact slap sound and see if I could move the bed of the 998 at all. I wasn't anywhere close. Then the SGT and I both tried simultaneously, and we would've been around 400+ with all our gear and our body weight. Still did not budge the ass end and still not that big BANG sound of whatever hit the bed of the humvee.

68

Another time when we'd patrol the east half of the property, we had a little hideaway nook in some of the high grass and cattails near a bit of a small wet and marshy area. This is where at two separate times, I had this vision of this HUUUUUGE werewolf bust through the high grass, grabbing me, and pulling me right out of the humvee through those shitty vinyl doors. Now, this all happened after the slap in the back of Rover East.

I had never heard of a Dogman at this time. Bigfoot, yes, but never a Dogman. I heard about them maybe ten years later from listening to Sasquatch Chronicles. So that was my weird encounter. It's just strange how we were in the middle of an empty lot and saw absolutely nothing. We even thought it could've been the 3rd shift messing with us, but we saw nothing and nobody. We'd even do a dismounted shoreline patrol along Lake Ontario with our NVGs and I never felt anything along that trail through the woods when we dismounted.

After doing some research and knowing people that live out that way, there are a lot of typical Dogman signs and activities. Howls, growls, baby crying sounds, sightings... a lot of crazy stuff. I wish I were researching these cryptids then like I am now. Oh, and to clear up the Dogman image I was getting was while awake and on duty. I've heard other stories where Dogmen have done some image projecting on someone while they're awake. So that's basically what I experienced.

Fort Indiantown Gap

My Ex used to tell me while he was sleeping, that he saw a man or figure standing next to the bed or in the corners of the room. He often saw a "man with a mustache". I don't know who it could have been, but anyway... Fast forward to another annual training, we had some free time one day, and most of us decided to go back and take naps in the barracks.

The girl in the bunk next to me was asleep for about an hour when she woke up and asked me if she had been screaming. I said no... you didn't say anything the whole time. You were sleeping. She said she just had sleep paralysis and thought she was awake.

In her "awake dream," she was in the same barracks with us, but we were all staring at her. But the thing that got me... she said there was a 'man with a mustache' standing next to my bunk. He was bent over and was the only person looking at me instead of her. She's a complete skeptic, and I had never told her about what my Ex saw too.

Fort McCoy Compass Course 1A

During a night land navigation exercise, I was out on Compass Course 1A, and I was walking down one of the two-track trails that were out there. Immediately as I rounded the corner off the road to the trail, I felt the hairs on the back of my neck stand up like I was being watched. So, I kept on walking, but I could hear something mirroring my footsteps

After a while, I did the old hunter's trick of stopping abruptly while walking to see if something was following me. Sure as shit, I heard a few more footsteps after I stopped walking myself.

I tried this maybe three or four times, and I was freaked the fuck out. I ran into another person out on the trail, and he swore he was being followed by something too.

So, we began walking as we had found our points and we both still felt like we were being watched. About five minutes after we linked up, we heard this grunting noise from the woods, and a huge animal took off and cleared a lot of land up Pikes Peak very quickly.

A whole bunch of other guys on that course reported the same thing. I've been hunting my entire life, and I've never been afraid of the woods. I barely heard its footsteps following me. The only rational thing I could think of was maybe it was a mountain lion or something stalking us, but I really don't know.

The Border

Currently assigned to the border mission, where I have seen what I believe to be a Skinwalker. It was night, with perfect illumination, and we were under NVGs. My team and I first sighted what appeared to be a black cat 60 meters from our position.

It was walking away from us, and being of no immediate concern, we ignored it. It's about 100 meters away when we go back to scanning our sectors. My buddy is scanning behind me when he tells me, "Dude, this cat grew."

I turn and shit you not it was a hog. I'd say it's about 50-80 lbs max, so decent sized. Maybe it scared away the cat, but now there was a hog where we last saw it. It stays away from us, not making any noise, just rooting around.

So we're joking around about dropping it. When it starts walking in circle patterns slowly making its way toward us. We decide to approach it. It turns as we come and walks a straight line away from us. We get a good look at the tracks, which match that of a hog. But the tracks were super deep. The ground is solid dirt, and these were about three and a half inches deep.

We chamber rounds are ready for anything when it stops about 25 meters in front of us in the shadow of a tree. We slow our walk and take another few steps towards it. At this point, we feel something off—kind of a bad vibe. We stop using NVGs and white light it.

It stands up ON ITS HIND LEGS AND STANDS AT MY HEIGHT. It was about six feet tall standing up. Eyes level with mine. Didn't make a sound. We run. But when we look back, it's vanished.

We booked it back to the Humvees and climbed on top. When we returned, our guys were confused and asked what had happened. They didn't believe us, but we warned the next shift to keep their eyes open. My driver and I considered emptying our mags into it, but we're on the border and wouldn't want to deal with the paperwork and questioning for firing rounds at something barely anyone believes in. We said the Lord's Prayer and for the rest of the shift sat on top of our humvees. First time I've been scared for a while.

Haunted HQ

I've worked at an old military hospital converted to a HQ/recruiting office. Lots of issues with the building. It's pretty old, pretty creepy, and derelict, especially on floor number three, where no lights are working.

I was tasked to work at the building, and first creepy note: elevators like to run and stop on floors without any input. On one such occasion was getting on the elevator and stopped on good old floor three for no reason, the door opened but would not close at all. I step out to see if I can call the other elevator, nothing

Look around and its pitch black. All I hear is light tapping down the hallway and noises all around. I try to look for a stairway in a pitch-black environment; as soon as I get far enough from the elevator door closes and leaves. I'm like fuck great, going to be here in the dark looking for an exit.

The tapping noise gets louder and pretty sure I hear a door open and close. Soon as that happens, I book it in the direction I'm assuming is the stairway, nope, just more noises. I can't tell what it is. Eventually, the elevator comes back randomly. I jump on and press any floor that would get me out.

Orchard TA

Yeah, so I'm in the reserves, and we go out to either Yakima Training Center or Orchard Training Area for AT. I've seen a lot of funky shit at Orchard while I was there, which wasn't that long ago.

The way we had a fireguard was one guy would operate the radio, and another guy would patrol the wire around the FOB. A lot of the time, I would hear movement and from the outside of the wire and see shadow figures clear as day because the whole training area is a flat desert.

If you looked at the shadow figures without your NVGs, they don't show up. But with them on you can see them move around at night and hear them. I never really brought it up to the other guys because that makes you seem like you're losing your shit, so a lot of the time I would ignore it.

I often would hear breathing that wasn't mine from outside the wire too. I usually hold my breath to see if it was mine, and the breathing would continue—just a lot of funky shit out there. My NVGs would often die out of nowhere despite having fresh batteries. I don't mean they would flicker off I mean they would just shut off.

It's on old Indian land, so as someone who is native it wouldn't surprise me if there were pissed-off native spirits who fuck with the units that go out there to train. Range control was also very, very strict about touching rock stacks and animal bones. Like not the normal strict, every brief there was always, "don't fucking touch the rock stacks and animal bones." If it looked like it was old native stuff, don't touch it.

Challenge and Password

It was autumn 2016 at Fort McCoy, WI. My buddy had taken his life at the beginning of the month. I hadn't known him as well as others, so I pushed my grief away thinking that I didn't have the right to be still grieving when people who knew him better seemed to be doing okay. Anyway, we're conducting an FTX, and I'm pulling the 02-03 watch shift on the last night. I'm barely keeping my head up, but I'm making it through.

About 3/4 of the way through, I hear rustling at the tree line and what sounds like footsteps. The BN CO had been bouncing around between the different companies on foot, so I figured it must've been him and gave them the challenge expecting the password. Nobody responded, but a figure appeared about 20 yards away. They didn't respond to my second challenge and began moving towards me. Before I could alert anyone, I recognized them as my buddy. I leaped up to my feet, thinking I must be hallucinating and need to wake up.

They were still there, just staring back at me. I asked them if it was them, but they just smiled, turned around, and walked back the way they'd come. I got back down into my position, thinking I must've been tripping from lack of sleep or something. But the other guy on shift had crawled over to my position and asked me who the guy in civilians had been. We were relieved shortly after that, but I just cried in my position until stand-to.

I haven't talked about this with anyone because I thought everyone would think I was crazy or something. I never got to say goodbye, and that experience helped me realize I need to grieve at least a little. A few months later, I was sent a video by a mutual friend taken a few nights before he passed, where he was drunkenly ranting about how awesome I was.

TRAINING

PVT Oliver
Drill Sergeant

1-81 AR BN OSUT Barracks. Not sure if anything else happened anywhere, but that was the only place I know of firsthand. Not sure where the name is from, but I referred to him as PVT Oliver, our resident ghost. If the privates ever saw or experienced anything, we'd tell them it was PVT Oliver. We were getting ready for a new cycle and were prepping a few days ahead. We were laying out TA50 to issue to the privates. The way we did that was to pack it all into a rucksack and place it on the bunks, so when they arrived all they needed to do was grab it and go.

Well it was two DSs and me laying out this gear. We started on one end and worked our way down to the other end. We placed the rucks alternating where the PVTs feet would be. We made it about a 3rd of the way down the bay. We left and grabbed some more rucks but when we came back, we noticed all the rucks were now at the side of the bed centered.

We all though the Senior DS had moved all the rucks, and figured they wanted them that way. We finished up and matched all the rucks to the position. A few days later the Senior approaches us and asks why we changed the position of the rucks. After back and forth we figured out that the Senior wasn't in the bay. In fact, all the Drills were outside the bay or at another part of the base.

We realized it was PVT Oliver up to no good.

Benning
Trainee

I went to the Benning School for wayward boys, basic and infantry school, back in 2012. I say this because, in the late summer of 2012, we were doing our final field exercise. Night three, we were in our patrol base and I remember one of the guys in an adjacent gun position coming over to ours.

He asked us if we had seen anything in the trees in front of us. We all flipped our NVGs down and looked out in the woods. We all saw something moving out there.

It just moved from tree to tree watching. We all had only maybe 15 hours under NVGs at this point. I just figured it was my inexperience with NVGs that I couldn't focus or pick out a human shape.

Reading all these stories lately made me think back to that. We saw blackish-grey under NVGs, it didn't have a fully human form, and it just moved from tree to tree every three to five minutes. It never came closer and finally left.

I never had any fear or dread. I distinctly remember the hair standing up on the back of my neck and a general unease as we all watched. No one said anything about it. After reading all this on your page, I know I was watching and being watched by some creature, not of this world. Or rather maybe an animal from the old times.

Fireguard
Trainee

I was there for basic training. Every night we took turns doing "fireguard." It's basically where two Soldiers rotate every hour to watch the door and make sure everyone stays in bed. There were four barracks bays. Ours, the female bay, was upstairs and across the hall from a male bay, but we used separate stairwells. Females and drill sergeants were the only ones using this center stairwell.

The drill sergeants would come up to check on us periodically. The doors were heavy and loud. We could hear when they went into the bay across the hall.

So now and then, we would hear footsteps come up the stairs and stop. Neither of the doors would open, and we'd never listen to them go back down. We even heard objects ROLLING DOWN THE STAIRS. You could hear them hitting every individual step as they went down. It was so scary.

After lights out, everyone had to stay in bed. We had to let the fireguard know if we were getting up to go to the bathroom, and no showering was allowed after that time. We would hear people talking in the bathroom in the middle of the night and sometimes hear the showers going.

So, we would look because we all would get in trouble if anyone were up making noise... but no one was in there. I should also mention, the lights are motion sensed. We would walk in, and the lights would turn on. A physical person hadn't been walking in there for at least a few minutes.

Our beds were in rows, all lined up. One night we all got woken up by a scream right next to our row of beds. All of us sat up simultaneously, freaking out and looking at each other. We couldn't figure out where it came from.

Sand Hill
Drill Sergeant

Fort Benning: Sand Hill is highly haunted. Suicides are a rarity, but the ghosts of Sand Hill are very mischievous. We had three in my company.

One in our 1st PLT Bay, one in our 3rd PLT Bay, and one in our Company that hated Drill Sergeants. I am sure it was Private because it would mess with us a lot. In the CP, if you turned off the lights, it would be BLACK in darkness. But you knew someone was there. It's that feeling.

Some of the biggest telltale signs were the dark figure in our kitchen which would watch you while you slept. The other one was the random motion sensor lights in the conference room going on and off, but the creepiest and disturbing were the sinks. It only ever happened when you were about to fall asleep.

The sinks, like our lights, are motion activated. It never happened in the daytime, but at night the sinks would go on and off randomly. The lights, however, only came on in the bathrooms if they wanted them to. We would usually have to wave vigorously to turn them on. This ghost had no problem, but it NEVER turned the sinks and lights on simultaneously.

One night, it was going crazy. Every five seconds, the sinks would come on. I wanted proof. My buddies all knew the CP was haunted as well. So, I pulled out my phone, and immediately the sinks stopped. As soon as I put my phone down, it would start. I started counting intervals. Kept my phone out for five minutes. Nothing. Put it away. The sink goes off.

Next time 12 minutes to offset. The sink doesn't go off. Goes in a pocket. The sink goes off. It didn't want to be caught on camera. Little bastard would always try to keep you awake. I never left the conference room or kitchen area doors open. Sinks are one thing but watching me is another.

3-11th BN Fort Benning
Officer Candidate

I don't have a full-blown story like your posts, just random short statements from other Officer Candidates regarding the 3-11th BN building/OCS footprint. Many of the Officer Candidates have been weirded out on the third floor, especially the bathroom.

When we have our staff duty shifts at BN, we have to do some cleaning and maintenance throughout the night. Basic stuff like sweeping, vacuuming, taking out the trash, etc.

The current OCS footprint is relatively new for OCS. I know that in the early 2000s, we used to be located down by the Airborne school. I know our buildings were once barracks for colored Soldiers during federal segregation, but I'm pretty uninformed about building history.

There are two Officer Candidates assigned to staff duty for 24 hours and one always needs to be at the desk. This means one of us has to go up to the second and third floors to clean alone.

The lights flicker in the bathrooms, and several Officer Candidates have mentioned that they've felt like they were being watched on the third floor. This may be because it's late, we're tired, and being alone makes you imagine things.

The most I've heard is just what sounded like knocking or footsteps. It's enough to keep me at the desk unless necessary. I like to believe it's just in my head, but others have said the same thing about the third floor unprompted.

Just the other month, some staff cleaned out the attic and found an old footlocker. This thing was ancient. It had a bunch of memorabilia from both WW1 and WW2, including personal letters. There are many old things hidden around the basement and attic that just have been forgotten. I'll ask around to see if anyone has anything more detailed. I don't have anything spectacular, that's why I wondered whether you've ever heard anything. The collective unease about the third floor at night made me wonder.

Land Nav Witch
Trainee

So, I went through the 22 weeks of infantry OSUT and the worst experience I had was the individual night land nav. I was in the middle of the swamp around 0200 looking at my map. Suddenly every hair on my body stood on end, and my red-light flickers. I turn it off and start looking around when I spot the silhouette of a woman in what I can only describe as a pioneer's outfit. I looked away for a second and looked back. Nothing. I told myself that I was seeing shit, picked a direction I thought was good, and started walking.

I started hearing the crunching and breaking of leaves in rhythm with my steps behind me as if someone was matching my pace, and my hairs stood up again. I stopped and looked behind me, nothing. I continued walking; the same thing happened. Looked again, nothing. I decided that three points was plenty for tonight and started booking it. As I'm running, I hear and see something jumping from tree to tree, keeping pace with me as I cut through the woods sprinting full speed.

I make it to the starting point, turn in my shit and sit on my gear. Another guy comes running in about 15 minutes later (we still have two hours left at this point, so it makes no sense why he would be in a hurry). He does his shit and sits next to me. He turns to me, "Dude... did you have a point in the swamp?"

I gesture at my boots and pants. "Yeah, can't you tell?"

"Yeah, sorry. but anyway... did you see a woman in a-"
"Pioneer outfit!"

"Yeah! I was writing down my point's info when my light started flickering, and I heard something in the tree above me. I looked up and saw her sitting in a tree up above the point, just staring down at me with lifeless eyes and an empty face. I ran faster than I ever have and didn't stop till I got here."

It's at this point where the guy sitting behind us leans forward, "You all saw her too?" We nod. " I started walking into the swamp when I saw her sit up out of the water and slowly turn to look at me. I froze and like... I only broke out of it when the LT walked up behind me and asked what I was looking at. I looked at him and pointed but when I did, she was gone. No noise, nothing." This kid was an honest dude, and I could tell by the look in his eye that he wasn't fucking with us.

Yankee North
Trainee

I had an experience in basic during individual night land nav. I'm unsure where others experienced the witch, but I was at the Yankee North course during the 22 weeks OSUT course.

Around 0200-0300, I had been to most of my points and was walking a hardball on the edge of the boundary. As I walked, I realized that I heard footsteps maybe 10m in the woods on the out-of-bounds side. At first, I thought it was just an animal, no big deal.

A few steps later, I was still hearing these footsteps; the problem was, they were keeping pace with me perfectly, but I would only hear maybe every four or five of my steps to its one. This suggested to me that whatever was walking alongside was very large.

My heart started racing at the thought of this, so I decided to pick up the pace. I started waking very fast, and the footsteps never lost speed. I started jogging, and they were still 10 m away. I started sprinting, and they were still landing every four of my steps to the left of me.

I never got a good look at what this entity was, nor did I have any intention to do so. I just kept moving and kept my eyes forward due to a sense of pure fear and dread. I was nearing the turn-off for my last point but decided I'd be better off just skipping my previous point since it was so close to where I am and kept running until I got back to the start point.

When I sat down, I asked a few guys if they walked the hardball at the edge, and two of them said they did. I wondered if they heard anything strange, and they described exactly what I heard. The hair on the back of my neck rose, and I didn't sleep well out there even though there were 200 of us.

I never saw what was hunting me, so maybe it could have been related. Either way, there is a lot of bizarre activity in those Georgia woods.

Fort Benning
Trainee

Where to start… I arrived there in July of 2013 and graduated on October 13. The first weird experience there was in 30th AG. During processing, we got put in brand new barracks. My processing company was on the 3rd floor.

I can remember that there was a bay on the other side of the floor that a sergeant said he saw a shadow figure come in and out of multiple times. Every time he saw it enter the bay, he said you could hear it open and slam wall lockers closed or knock them over.

So, I asked him if I could take a fire watch because I was curious to see if it was true. For most of the night, it was uneventful till about an hour before we changed fire watches. It started with wall lockers opening and slamming shut, and that went on for about five minutes, or so. I finally got the courage to take a look because I thought it was someone playing a prank.

So I opened the bay door and asked if anyone was in there. All I got in response was more wall lockers slamming shut. In typical stupid fashion, I told whatever it was to shut up. Then the shower turned on, and that was it. I had enough and walked out.

I had another experience with this light I was. The experience with the reddish-orange light was weird and confusing because myself and the four other guys who saw it tried to rule it out as maybe a flare or something. But when we asked our drill sergeants in the morning if anyone was shooting flares or if we had aircraft flying around they said no. To this day I still can't rule out what it was because it would do figure 8s or a rectangular pattern and it just disappeared.

I came back three hours later and the light was back doing the same thing until the sun finally came up. I honestly did not feel comfortable doing anything in those woods on that base. They had the creepiest vibe every time we went out to do a field exercise or a land navigation test.

West Point
Cadet

I have an experience related to room 4714 at USMA. One summer, I lived directly across from room 4714 in Scott Barracks. It was only my roommate and I on the same floor as 4714. None of the other rooms were occupied. One afternoon I was taking a shower after PT in the bathroom directly behind room 4714.

At one point, I hear the bathroom door open, and footsteps walk in. Thinking it was my roommate, I said "hi" but got no answer. The footsteps stop at the end of the bathroom, but I didn't hear them again.

Then all of a sudden, the room gets cold. Mind you. This is the middle of summer in upstate NY. It was usually about 90+ degrees out, humid, and the barracks didn't have air conditioning.

At this point, I'm a little weirded out and decide it's time to leave. When I opened the shower curtain to get my towel, it was just swinging by itself on the hook, and no one else was around. There was only one hallway in and out.

I grabbed my towel and got out of there as quickly as I could. I never saw anything, just heard and felt the presence of someone else, but there was no one there. One of the weirdest experiences of my life.

OSUT
Trainee

I graduated from OSUT on May 21st so take this cherry-ass boots word that this is fresh. The first time anything happened, no one knew until a holdover 12M talked to C Co whose barracks were across from us. The first night we got there at 0300, he was on fireguard and allegedly saw a featureless pitch-black figure standing at attention underneath the lit-up breezeway. He went to call someone, and it was gone.

1st PLT male bay would consistently have a shadow come up to the door between 0000 and 0330 and move away. It also didn't trigger the motion sensor lights. Everyone saw that shit. We had one G-Shock watch taped to the desk because we weren't allowed watches. The first time we talked about it on fireguard, it flickered on and off for 15 seconds. G Shocks don't do that.

Week 13, I was in the restrooms, and the same 12M holdover was reading a book on the shower bench, and I heard a shower curtain violently slam to one side, and 12M go, "Oh shit!". I rush out and look and obviously no one. Any time we would talk about it, the lights would flicker. Stairs constantly had footsteps running up and down with no one in them.

Hands In The Brush
Trainee

I also went to Fort Jackson, and while rucking to an area where we could set up for the night after night, there was a trail we went that got tight. So, we were all squeezed together, and when my eyes adjusted: I saw what looked like hands reaching out of the thick brush that was on either side of the trail.

I thought I was hallucinating from sleep deprivation, but later during the FTX, a few battles and I saw things moving around in the woods silently between trees and poking heads out to look at us. Humanoid dark shapes moving between the trees. Then the heads would poke out behind trees for a little bit.

The following day we talked to others to see if anyone else had anything weird happen that night, and I think we found five or six other people who had at some point during the Forge seen something odd in the woods. Honestly, if anything, it might be Civil War ghosts or a curse of the land from natives or even witches. It wouldn't surprise me.

B Co 1-50
Trainee

So, here's my story, as well as some encounters that some other dudes had. At Benning, we were at B Co 1-50.

Our first couple of weeks there, we didn't experience anything. But as time went on, whatever was there was getting more and more pissed at us.

The first occurrence that I can remember was two guys on fireguard were playing with the NVGs that we just got issued. They both saw a shadow figure at the end of the bay go from the bathroom across the bay and disappear into the wall lockers, they both confirmed that they saw it.

One of my close buddies who didn't have sleep paralysis started getting it. There was a dark figure at his bunk and it would sometimes hurt him in his sleep.

One of the regular occurrences was at night, a latrine stall door slamming. Whenever it would happen, I would watch to see if someone would come out, but no one ever did. The scariest shit that personally happened to me was when I went to take a piss, washed my hands under my red lens, and heard the stall door slam. My first reaction was that I thought someone else was there, but then I heard flip-flops.

Still, nobody was there, then the shuffling turned into running towards me, and I bolted. I left the water running and never went back into the restroom at night without turning ample light on.

"Keep your eyes open"
Officer Candidate

Got an OCS one. We were at OCS in Fort Benning, Ga. This was January 2019 and doing our 2-1/2 weeks in the field for STX. We set up each night up the road from a training facility that would play the Muslim call to prayer each night around 0230. Across the street from us was an empty field.

Another guy and I were told to be gate guards one night and make sure no one came into our makeshift FOB from 0200-0300. Call to prayer plays. Zero cars came past us up to this point. After it finishes, we see a guy walking up the road towards us.

He was wearing shorts, a t-shirt, and flip-flops in 20-degree weather at Ft. Benning on a weekday. Immediately a car comes flying down the road in the opposite direction. Lights sort of hit him but the car passes him, and the guy walking disappeared not even 30 yards from us.

We freak out. Immediately radio the TOC. The cadre on duty came out and walked into the open field. He was gone for over 15 minutes. He came back and said to us: "I uhh… I didn't see anything... Keep your eyes open." But he couldn't hide the spooked look on his face.

"He just got silent."
Trainee

I was at basic training at Fort Leonard Wood. We had one guy in our company that just never got along with anyone. He did weird stuff like talk to trees and talk about being a witch. Literally the man would sit alone and whisper to the trees.

Well, one guy talked shit and said he was faking it and this dude said, "okay, I'm going to curse you" (I know this shit sounds insane, but weird stuff happened after).

After this, we started hearing a little girl running around the bay. We would listen and hear a child running around at all hours of the night

The person who he cursed started waking up at the same time every single night. Always 0300. He would sleepwalk into the laundry room act like he was opening a vent. He would always be saying, "it's okay, you can come out now." He would then walk to a side room on the other side of the bay and say, "it's okay, you can be free."

Now, this shit freaked out the whole bay for a while. We even asked our DS if the building was haunted, and he just got silent. I know this story sounds insane, but I swear on my life, it happened.

Imposters On The STX Lanes
Officer Candidate

I was OCS, and the dreaded STX lanes came up. It was early on in the week, so we felt pretty rested before we settled into the patrol base for the long night of 50% security. Around 0200, we started hearing coyotes, which sounded like a whole band of them making that unnerving yippy noise. That wasn't uncommon in Fort Benning. Wildlife regularly stumbled across our PB, but this time it gave me chills up my spine. It sounded like they were circling us.

A couple of peaceful and silent minutes pass. The student Platoon Leader started checking security, making sure everyone who was supposed to be awake was awake. When he came back, a man was leaning against a tree. Thinking it was an Officer Candidate, he

86

started asking, "Hey OC, what are you doing standing?" No response, then it dawned on him, he just checked the whole gun line, and everyone was present and accounted for in their positions. "Who are you? What are you doing here?" He asked with still no response.

If you know anything about PB's, you'll know it's one way in and one way out, and a password guards it. There was no way some rando could get in without knowing the password, and there was no way 50% security would have missed him walking through. All of a sudden, the man started walking straight out of the OP. All I remember was he had very heavy footsteps. After that, I saw something in the forest. It would move between bushes and stare at us.

The following day we got back to the "TOC," and I noticed the cadre that was present all night had a cot set up, and he looked like he had just woken up. I was pretty close with this guy, so I asked him, "hey man were you fucking with us last night?" He responded, "hell no, it was way too cold. I was sleeping in the ammo shed". Then we asked around to the other platoons if they were fucking with us.

No one could even point out where we were that night. I don't know what it was or how it got there. That's it, that's the story. I'm not embellishing anything or making shit up. That's just what happened. Like most real-life events, I never got answers or any big reveal, so it's just going to remain unanswered for the rest of my life.

I was manning the 249 at the apex, so I just heard him stomping. The PL described him as tall, about 6'3" (which is weird because none of our cadre was over 6'), and the only other guys above 6'3" were one other dude who was a gate guard and me. The PL said he stunk, but I don't chalk it up to anything. After all, we all stink in the field. It was wearing a neck gaiter and a PC (which was also weird because we wore helmets). Important to know, neck gaiters were not authorized for wear at all. This was during COVID, and it was also strange he would cover his face walking alone in the forest. Also, his flag was on the wrong shoulder, and it was also an IR Flag (not authorized unless your cadre). That was how I was able to see him at first. He didn't wear a uniform patch either (we wore the infantry school patch). I would catch glimpses of something from the bushes. He moved weirdly like it was uncomfortable walking on two feet.

I don't know what it could have been. I grew up in Flagstaff, AZ. Skinwalker territory. The Navajo are adamant that Skinwalkers only existed inside their tribe. But shapeshifter stories are pervasive down in Georgia too. I'm not sure who or what it was, but it seemed like it was impersonating a Soldier and getting a lot of things wrong. I think they got like the goat man or some other type of thing.

All I know is Skinwalkers are people, medicine men, who practice dark things to intimidate people they don't like. Whether you believe they shapeshift at all, they do exist. Skinwalker is more of a practice than a cryptid. The lore goes deeper and supernatural, but most rational Navajo stop at that point.

Skinwalkers are simply humans trying to be animals. This was different. It was like something was TRYING to be human and failing pretty bad. Maybe it's my background or something. I don't know. But it just seemed off, that uncanny valley shit. I don't think there's a cryptid on the books to describe it. But I do think there's a reason why the uncanny valley evolved in humans. A lot of people hear these stories of creatures chasing them that seem…off. And most go, "oh, Skinwalker." But that's not accurate enough.

What I'm describing is more like a predator that evolved from us. It uses its intellect to lure and kill humans. It learns from speaking to us, it tries to understand our tribal mentality. I don't think they're shapeshifters. I think they're like mimics. It's hard to get evidence for them because they're exactly like us, but if you look at serial killers, their pathology and brain chemistry are just way different. Maybe it's part of that mutation that made these things.

Fort Knox
Cadet

Cadet Summer Training, I was in a patrol base walking the line on fireguard. A buddy and I were walking together, keeping each other awake and company.

We hear from the other side of the patrol base an ear-piercing scream. It sounded like the muffled scream of a woman like someone was being kidnapped. We ran over, and found the other four on fireguard, they all heard the same scream.

We were all convinced it was human until someone told us about fox calls. We took a preliminary look around but couldn't find anything strange, even with white light so we decided to call it.

The rest of the time in the field, I always felt like I was being watched, not in the "I'm in the field, there's OPFOR around" more like "always looking over my shoulder" kind of way.

Now on the outside, it wouldn't leave my head. The scream just played over and over, so I looked up what a fox call is like, and it wasn't anything close. It was a woman's scream 100%.

Tree Knocks At Knox
Cadet

Not anything impressive, but the summer I was at Fort Knox for Cadet Summer Training, I heard two massive logs being crashed against each other repeatedly one night while we were trying to sleep. We were on a patrol base. I wasn't trying to investigate.

Either some cadet was having a total mental breakdown, or something else was hitting those pieces of wood together. Went on for 30 minutes.

But like nobody in their right mind would do that for thirty minutes. It was far enough away to echo but was super loud. But like a big branch hitting another piece of wood. Very possible it could have been cadre messing with us, but it just didn't seem right.

Benning UFO
Trainee

We were out on an FTX towards the end of October, nice and cold out. So I'm in my fox hole with a battle buddy just wrapped up in a woobie, trying not to fall asleep.

He is conked out at the time as we were switching off. I happen to look up at the stars in my NVGs and see a ball of light moving towards us.

It looks like a plane, so I don't think much of it but watch it because it's something to keep me awake. As it nears us, it completely stops.

Then it hovers for a few moments before flashing off at what I could only describe as warp speed from a Star Trek movie or something. Gone in a flash and with a small trail behind it. No sounds whatsoever. Wild.

Haunted Benning
Trainee

So for both stories, this was at Fort Benning in 2014. The platoon bay we were in was pretty well acknowledged to be haunted, and just about everyone on fire watch saw the shadow people. We had one guy stationed at one end of the bay and then another on the far end, and every night you would see multiple shadow people moving in between the lockers and bunks. Eventually, we just got used to it and tuned it out.

But they would get aggressive sometimes as I woke up once getting my foot yanked on, or another time to the whole rack shaking. Only to look and see both of the guys on fire watch at their posts. Another guy got his blanket yanked off of his bed in the middle of the night.

Another great one that didn't happen to me but a buddy from another platoon. The CQ desk was facing out of the company area towards a very dense wood line, well one night at zero dark thirty he hears the most horrifying and unnatural screaming ever coming from that wood line for about five minutes and then it just stops. Others had listened to some soft crying coming from there too.

The Anvil
Trainee

So this was during The Anvil at BCT at Fort Jackson. My battle and I were doing our patrol around the hill to ensure everyone was where they were supposed to be. Anyways we got done with that and got to our fixed position.

After a while of sitting there, I started seeing heads peek out from behind the trees. I thought I was hallucinating until my battle asked if I saw them too. We saw them popping out from at least a dozen trees. The following day we were talking to a few people, and they asked us if we saw things in the trees too.

At Saint Lo, you'd always get the uneasy feeling that something was watching you. Sometimes you'd even hear leaves crunching when no one else was around. You'd also hear footsteps stomping around in the bricks at night; up and down the hallways and in your room. But when you looked, there was no one there.

Fort Benning: Terror Of A Different Breed
Trainee

The first incident was my sleep paralysis in the barracks at 30th AG. I never had it before in my life, and then the third or fourth night I was on Benning, I got it. I've had it multiple times since then. I remember waking up with the usual sleep paralysis symptoms, and dark energy took the shape of a toddler boy in the corner of the room (drifting above the lockers). It felt like the power of my body was flowing directly to it.

The second incident was night land nav. We were out in the weeds, how it usually gets. Middle of November and coming into the coldest winter that town has had in decades. We're trying to find our point when we suddenly hit a patch of crazy humidity and heat. We start hearing (not too far off from us) a low growling. I didn't stick around long, but a kid in my squad was super religious. He started calling on Jesus while we all got the fuck out.

The last incident was on fire watch. Me and my buddy were doing whatever you do on fire watch, and out of nowhere the entire building starts shaking as if an Apache was landing on the roof. It wasn't abnormal to hear the birds flying around at night, but this one was so loud it was as if it was right outside our door. The strangest part to me is that as loud as it was, not a single person stirred or woke up. Nobody else heard it but my buddy and I. That's the only reason I consider that a paranormal experience. I still think about that one often. What the hell could it have been?

Cherry Hall
Cadre

I did a 24-hour commo/weapon guard shift at the Cherry Hall (where all the classrooms, cadre office, and TOC are). I'm chilling playing Xbox in the TOC at 0245. A guard change happens where the students had a three-hour guard shift to guard their weapons.

The first LT comes up, signed him in, and waits for his buddy when I hear footsteps coming down the hall. They come down the hall, and right before they get to the TOC, they stopped. I and the LT looked at each other, and the LT went out in the hall thinking it was his buddy, not knowing where to sign in.

He rushes back, "no one is out there." I and the LT walk around the hall in both directions trying to see where he went thinking a prank was being played. It's past 0300 now, and the LT calls him. His buddy says, "Oh my bad, I'm running a little late I'll be pulling up in a few minutes."

Lost In The Woods
Officer

So a group of us go to Fort Leonard Wood to take a course. We get put up in these older National Guard barracks near basic training land. We have two females with us that got put in a different building not too far away.

The first night at 0100, we heard a knock on the back door and the voice of a female Soldier outside—one of the guy's answers, and no one is there. A few hours later, same knock, same voice. A different guy answers the door. This time the guy who answers the door sees (but not very well because it's dark out and snowing) a female in shorts and a short-sleeve shirt walking away from the building.

Again, it's below freezing and snowing. She doesn't answer when he calls out and disappears in the dark. It could easily be dismissed as one of the guys tried to get a tinder hookup and didn't work out, but weird stuff kept happening. The next night, a guy was sleeping in an individual room in the corner of the open bay. He wakes up to piss, and comes back to his room. As he gets within view of his door, sees a female walk into his room. He goes into his room to see who it is. No one is there.

The third night, we are all downstairs messing around, playing cards. Hear someone upstairs, walking heavily. Everyone is downstairs, either playing or watching. I go upstairs to see who is up there. Check the whole area, no one there. There were no stairs on the outside of the building that led upstairs. I slept upstairs that entire trip, and each night it sounded like someone would walk up the stairs and walk past my room but never saw anyone walk by. I could also hear every time someone got up to piss and could see them walk down and back up the stairs since my bed was in the corner near the stairs.

We also heard whispers and a female voice in the building while we were there. Also, additional weird detail, when the girls checked into their barracks room, no one else was supposed to be staying in it. However, we did find a ruck full of clothes, gear, and personal items near a bed in the corner. The entire time we were there (2 weeks), no one came by to grab it, and it never appeared to be disturbed. Not super scary but very weird that 20 people experienced the same odd occurrences.

UFO Over Fort Benning
Trainee

In basic I was "pulling security" during the night of our first FTX when I look over to right to see another trainee rolled on his back laying on his back star gazing, I thought he was going to get us fucked up but quickly forget when he told us he was staring at some sort of UFO.

He guided us in, under the moon and to the left of a tree there was a dot, about in brightness of a planet but it looked like a star. It moved around periodically, sometimes changing position in the sky. Once disappearing behind the tree and coming back out, never moving more than a small distance away from its original starting position. Then after about 20 minutes it moved steadily to one direction before picking up speed and darting into the distance, never to be seen again. It had no color; it has no blinking effect and we never heard a sound.

UFO Over Fort Leonard Wood
Trainee

Was out in the field doing drivers training with 113's for the company with one of the crusty PSG's. Did the day training all was good so we moved on to the night portion with NVG's around about midnight.

We all took a smoke break and we're looking at the stars. As we were looking up maybe 500 feet above our heads all the stars were distorting slowly. It looked like a slow flying invisible plane was flying above us warping the stars view around it. Really creepy shit.

It was a group of about 25 of us there and most everyone saw it. It was there and gone within about 30 seconds. No one knew what it was, and it made no sound. That was about four years ago on the back side of Leonard Wood. Still got no clue. Wouldn't say paranormal but definitely weird.

FORT POLK

Whiskey Cheeto

This was early 2006 at Fort Polk. I was in a G-Man up against the Rotational Training Unit (RTU). They had taken Shugart Gordon, and our squad was tasked with making diversionary attacks from the south for a couple of days. So we worked them over, hitting from MPRC lanes and south of Self Village.

Well, we were told to go hang out at Whisky Cheeto Inn for the day and to push Shugart at 0200 that night. We made it to Whiskey Cheeto no issue and hung out all day with the two vans and the Tech V. No one was in this little village except for us. So we played around all day. We were screwing around in the tunnel system and the empty buildings.

Night fell, and everyone simmered down, and we all chilled at the fire pit. We sent the joes to rest around 2100 because we would roll at 0100. My buddy and I stayed up, pulling security, playing with the fire, and telling lies about drinking out in Houston. It was around 2300-0000 when suddenly three or four of the windows on the three-story building started to slam.

I'm not talking about wind slamming but like someone slamming them. We looked at each other, and I said I would check it out. So, I went to the doorway and started yelling, thinking it was RTU, that we would kill them all. Then something laughed at me. I heard it, and my buddy heard it. We went and woke everyone up and started searching the area. No one found or saw anything.

One of the privates went to the tunnel system entrance and swore he heard voices coming from it like someone was down there freaking out. So, we all piled into the tunnel system. Nothing. On the way out, we heard laughing again. At this point, we all freak out.

Load up in the vehicles and rolled to Shugart.

We never went back to Whiskey Cheeto after that. We all swore something was out there, and to this day, we all believe someone or something was fucking with us. To this day, I think it was dead Soldiers who came back here. Who else would have fucked with us like that? It's fuck fuck games we play with each other

The Return To Whiskey Cheeto

Ok, so this was ten years after the 1st experience at Whiskey Cheeto. I'm out of the Army and decided to move back to Polk to become a fire marker. So, being the new guy, they left me in some pretty shitty spots watching IEDs or in areas where G-man or BLUFOR wasn't shooting. As time went on and they realized I was a decent fire marker, I started to get put in the cool guy spots.

Early spring 2016, I was on night shift and got placed down at Whiskey Cheeto because BLUFOR was getting hammered there all day by Geronimo with indirect fires. So, of course, when I get down there BLUFOR is all dead and gone. I remember my last time down at Whiskey Cheeto and said fuck that. So, I went to the radio tower and building with an outside light to hole up for the night.

I'm sitting on my four-wheeler listening to all the radio traffic and fighting going on in Bakor when my radio cuts out. I went to get a new battery from my lunch box when I swear, I heard laughing and giggling. I didn't respond because fire markers don't exist in rotation—plug in the new battery and nothing.

The laughing starts again, but this time it sounded like a bear laughing and loud AF. So, I yell back into the darkness for whoever is playing games to shut the fuck up, or they'd catch an airburst round in the face. The laughing stops, and I go back to trying to unfuck the radio.

I get it back on after I plugged in my third battery, do a radio check, and go back to scanning the fight. Nothing is happening at this point, so I pull out a book I've been reading and sit there snacking and reading. I'm a couple of chapters in when my headlamp goes out. So back to my lunch box for more batteries.

As I'm digging for my AAAs, I hear what sounds like BLUFOR running down the road. I look up and down the street, and nothing is moving, and it's DEAD silent. The hairs on my neck stand up, and just outside the range of the light, I see movement. I pull up my PVS 7's and start scanning. I kept seeing shadows jump around and move too fast to be human, but I could never make out a firm shape.

I dive back into the pyro box, grab an airburst round and the pyro pistol. I load the pyro pistol and remember yelling, "You want to play fuck fuck games!?!?!! Let's play fuck fuck games". The movement stops, the noises stop, and my headlamp kicks back on. I start getting calls on the radio about five minutes later asking me to verify an IED out on Lane Charlie.

I go check in with G-man, and sadly they didn't have everything to make their IED work. I asked them before I left if they had anyone down at Whiskey Cheeto and they told me that all the G-men down there went back to Shugart. They even called the guys in Shugart to make sure that no one was down at Whiskey Cheeto.

I made my way back to my hole-up area and sat there the rest of the night reading with my loaded pyro pistol. When I came in that morning, I told the assistant branch manager, that if they EVER put me down at Whiskey Cheeto again: I'd shoot the shift leader with the pyro pistol and him. They never put me down there again.

"Imagine if you will…"

Imagine if you will: you're on night 2/2 of land navigation out at JRTC for validation. You've been listening to the suspicious rustles of wild horses and the rhythmic "meep meep meep" of the hogs while the deafening echo of the insects fills the rank, wet air.

You don't know how it gets hotter at night than it did during the day, but here you are, drowning on dry land, cuts and scrapes line your cheeks as you bust ass to what SHOULD be your last point. When all of the sudden your foot brushes up against something… solid.

It feels like a tree, but you can't feel one with your arms. A stump, maybe? You reach down and feel a solid anthill the size of a mortar round but something is strange. These aren't ants. They are not furiously swarming out to bite you.

Instead, you recoil and note that all that noise, all that air, all that JRTC experience has just… stopped. It's cold now. Silent too. You starting to get a bad feeling in the pit of your stomach but you are a goddamn AMERICAN Soldier! YOU are the thing that goes bump in the night! You are a barrel-chested attack dog for the American Freedom and you WILL NOT be deterred.

That point should be right in front of you, but there's nothing but a clearing. There is… something in the middle though. Maybe the point box got knocked down? Maybe some dickhead before you put it on the ground? Whatever. Better go check it out.

But it's not a point. It's not a little staple puncher. It's a pile. A lone standing pile of bones of various sizes, shapes, and species. Your rational brain knows this can be anything. Maybe Cletus and Boudreaux have their fire pits here. Maybe some edge lord Soldiers drag their pest control victims here. Maybe… maybe, but you can't seem to shake that awful feeling inside of your and the deafening silence of the area isn't helping.

For some reason you decide to quietly re-trace your steps back out the clearing, back through the brambles and brushes, back though the broken brush. But then it hits you. Like a break from the grave, just as you pass the empty anthill, you hear it.

A deathly, croaking moan like a Cheyenne-stokes death rattle comes leering out from right behind your head and fills your nose with the acrid smell that should have been in the pit.

You run for your life down the path you came in on, but as soon as you pass the anthill, everything is back to normal. Your hit with that awful wetness, the buzzing of bugs, and the orchestra of leadership doing a sweep for the stragglers. You're at a loss for what the fuck just happened.

You swore you've only been in the dreaded clearing but a minute. You should have like what, an hour left right? You can't seem to explain it but everyone is back at the patrol base and their watches are all 47 minutes ahead of yours.

The Box Witch Strikes

So for context, I'm in the 82nd and my company got tasked to play OPFOR at Polk. So we are not Polk natives nor experienced with the swamps of Louisiana. So fast forward ten days of active patrolling as OPFOR. Hunting BLUFOR in the swamps, draws, villages, you name it. We're on our last river crossing staged to intercept a company of Red Devils that should be coming out of the swamp.

We set up a blocking position and waited. We wait for the whole day, and nothing happens. That night we decide to start sending patrols into the swamp to find them. My fellow team leader and I volunteered to take the first patrol. Set the standard, that sort of thing. We pick a spot two water crossings away—easy thirty-minute patrol along the road.

We set out at around 2200, and it's pretty light-hearted and chill. My buddy and I cross our first water point with no problem. We continue walking uphill for about a click. This was when things got weird. After walking uphill, we start walking down and fast.

At first, I didn't think anything of it, but as we walked down, we stopped joking with each other. The crickets and cicadas stopped making noise. The forest somehow got darker. As we neared the bottom, I looked at my boy, and he instantly locked eyes with me. I told him I felt like we were about to get ambushed. He told me he felt like we were being watched since we crested the hill.

Now we're sketched out, but we assume it's the BLUFOR we're looking for. As we near the water crossing, it's dead silent. So eerily quiet you can hear your heartbeat. Feel it behind your eyes, and you start to sweat. We get down there and start IR lazing everything we can, hoping someone shoots at us so we can get the hell out of there. Nothing, not a single thing in that swamp moved. It made no sense. Where did the animals and bugs go? A swamp surrounded us on both sides of this bridge. I spot something weird under IR, and we agree it's probably an LP/OP.

He pulls out a star cluster, and I observe. He bangs this thing five times. It doesn't light. Now everything feels wrong. Every nerve in my body is on edge. Everything about the situation felt wrong. He resorts to smacking it on the ground. It launches high in the sky. We both raise our weapons and watch the swamp. It starts casting shadows. Even now, I don't know what happened next. All I remember was every fiber of my being said run. Run, or you're not leaving this swamp.

Then a sound that sounded like a log smacking another log bounced off the swamp. Something heavy and oversized started charging at us. My buddy darted back uphill, and I was on his ass. I've never run so hard in my life. We ran until we crested the hill again, and on cue, the sounds of nature returned.

I didn't feel like I was being watched anymore. I could breathe again. I looked at my buddy, and he shook his head at me. I told him, "Bro, that wasn't a fucking deer. I know that wasn't." He told me not to say its name. We went back to our blocking position with cold sweats. We both agreed not to speak about what we saw. We also changed the route, so no one had to go over that hill.

It was big, and at first I thought, "oh man, that's a big deer." But it didn't sound like a deer. The noises it made as it broke tree trunks and limbs assured me that it was a not a deer. I wish I still knew what water crossing it was, but we were in the northwest. It sounded like if someone took a big hollow metal pole and started whacking trees while crushing tree branches. But the stomps were so loud and heavy.

Shadowy Figures In Marwandi

I've been 1-509th Geronimo OPFOR for two years now and spent enough time in the box. During a jump, I finished my second point of performance, and I looked below me for other jumpers (at this time, there's no one but medics on the DZ).

I saw about 6-9 extremely tall figures around where I was going to land. With approximately 250 ft left, I lowered my ruck down the lowering line, and they scattered. During another jump, I saw the exact tall figures again—at least three more watching me fall into the DZ.

Fast forward, I was in one of the small towns (I think Marwandi), and we were hunkering down for the night. I was on second shift for pulling security while everyone was sleeping in the building was racked out. I was already tired as fuck from TICs with RTU, so I was getting woozy.

About an hour into my shift, I heard movement around the building, so I started looking out windows. I looked out a window and saw a figure on the other side. So, I immediately rushed over to it with my weapon up, thinking it was RTU. When I looked out the window, it was gone.

Then when I turned around, a large black figure was standing at the other end of the building (this is under NVGs, by the way) and it proceeded to sprint directly at me. I shat myself and lifted my NVGs, and it was gone. But I could feel air push past me like something did run past me.

My other two team members in the room jumped up and asked me why I was sprinting across the building. I told them it wasn't me, and they thought I was losing my mind. Maybe I was hallucinating, maybe not. But every time we roll pass that building, I still get uneasy.

The Box Witch

We were doing JRTC, and the first time I had ever heard of "The Box Witch" was from a not very well-liked corporal. He would always joke about the Box Witch stealing things like gear, knives, gloves, eye pro, etc.

I thought maybe it was an excuse for people to use the black hand, but I heard rumors before going out by some of the seasoned dudes that the Box Witch was real. I laughed it off. I didn't think much of it.

Atropia [JRTC], the talk, and chatter continue about the Box Witch. I still just shrugged it off. Well, finally we got out there. We hadn't seen or heard anything abnormal or paranormal for the first two weeks, but then we went to the little village "Tofani," and we were ordered to hold the town from OPFOR.

Well, around 0230-0300, it was my turn for firewatch. So, I slid my NVGs on and got my weapon, stood out on the little roof access area we had. I heard this blood-curdling scream. It sounded close, so I woke up the team leader, and he thought I was playing a prank until he heard it too. We sent two manned foot patrols out about 300m to circle the village and check for any signs of OPFOR.

I was with my team leader when we heard the scream again, and he stopped dead in his tracks. I asked him what was wrong. Still, he shook his head, he urged us to hurry our foot patrol and head back to the village. I saw shadows move in my NVGs, and I alerted him with distance and direction. The only description I could place was movement.

He had me pop bipod and got behind a tree for cover. We waited. We could see the rustling of bushes getting closer and closer, but something wasn't sitting right. I couldn't see anyone, the rustling was right in front of me in the bushes, but I couldn't see anything, my blood started running cold.

I was petrified. I felt like I couldn't move. All I could feel was my team leader's hand on my back, picking me up with force and making me move. I still hope I was mistaken, but that instance leaves me blank. I can't draw a logical conclusion for not seeing anyone at all.

I think it was the Box Witch. I didn't see anyone the whole time we were at Tofani. Even stranger, the OC/Ts told us there was no OPFOR out that night.

Never Follow The Little Girl's Voice

Alright. Fort Polk. We were tasked with supporting some Special Forces at Fort Polk in 2016 during JRTC. They came into our room and said, "Hey, who wants to go raid an OPFOR position?" I raised my hand and jumped out of my cot.

They said to meet them outside in 2030. It was 1945. Oddly enough, I was the only volunteer. We were all smoked from constant missions. It was the very end of the cycle, but I couldn't miss working with actual Green Berets.

My friends loaded me up with their extra magazines and made sure that my MILES system was working correctly, and I went outside to smoke a cigarette. I was 10 minutes early for the Green Berets in the middle of Atropia.

I'm standing there smoking and hear a little girl crying. I've never seen a child there, and the civilians are long gone at this point. So I go and follow the little girls' voice. The next thing I know, I have two of my buddies carrying me. A third friend is behind them with my weapon.

The SF guys walked into our building and said, "Hey, where's [Anon]?" And my Platoon Sergeant responded, "he went outside to meet y'all." They said I was nowhere to be found, which escalated to the whole troop hunting for me.

I don't remember a goddamn thing about anything other than walking across the street to check on that girl. It was like I heard her voice, crossed the road where I thought I'd heard her, and then blacked out. I don't know what it was. I wasn't drinking. I don't have any history of blacking out, I don't know. It weirds me out.

Nightcrawler

In 2018 I was at JRTC to do medical coverage for a unit from the 101st, so I got to stay at the camp at Peason Ridge. It was 0300 and I was driving to their live fire. We were going with our lights off because we were still technically in the box, so we needed to use light discipline. But the moon was full and bright, so we didn't need NVGs. Soon we came around this bend in the road.

My Soldier and I both saw this fucking "thing" that was like a white polar bear. It looked like it was covered in white fur. The full moon made it look like it was glowing. It quickly hit us that this wasn't a bear. It was walking in a crouched position, it looked like a short man. But it had no clothes on, and just looked… wrong.

It was walking away from us, when I guess it must have realized we were behind it. It turned its head and looked at us. It made eye contact with me, then it stood up, and dead sprinted into the woods.

It was freakishly fast, too fast to a be a person. It stood upright like a person, but it was too short to be a person and again, this thing just looked... wrong.

My Soldier and I kept driving in a stunned silence. We were frozen in fear from the shock of what we just saw. We didn't say anything to each other and didn't speak until the sun came up. Finally, I said, "what the fuck was that?" He responded, "I'm not religious, but that was unholy" and we just dropped it at that.

"She's real."

It was my first time at JRTC. We were pulling security IVO Smith Villa (South West Corner of Geronimo DZ).

The whole night we all kept hearing whispers, footsteps coming up from behind us, and fingernails tapping on the glass windows of HMMWVs. We heard a scream come from the wood line. We sent a squad in to investigate. Never found what was screaming.

About two years later, I was back. I was somewhere around Barry DZ. It was a full moon that night. I remember thinking that there was no sound. Not just that, it was quiet. Like literally no sound.

I looked into a clearing and saw the silhouette of a human. I looked back with my NVGs and didn't see anything. I flipped my NVGs off and saw it again. After a second or two, it just kind of evaporated.

I'm not superstitious, spiritual, or even religious, but I believe in the Box Witch. I don't care what anyone says. She's real.

Not Much Of A Story

This isn't much of a story, but I was driving down a long road outside Polk. It was 0400 in the morning and foggy. The woods surrounded the road. I went through a section of the road where the fog was clearing up and saw it.

There was a Skinwalker clear as day right beside my car. Suppose I had to guess, around 10ft tall with a head that looked like a deer and long skinny arms easily bigger than the average man. It was walking the same way I was driving and looked over its shoulder right at me as I was going past.

My heart started beating super-fast, and I sped up until I was out of the woods. I don't believe in that stuff, but I saw what I saw. I only caught a glimpse and I still second-guess what I saw. I've never felt fear like that before. I'll admit it seems a little far-fetched, but there's something off about that area, and I don't intend on going back through that road anytime soon.

Tales From JRTC

[At JRTC] You just see random heat signatures out there. One time I saw a dude in the middle of the lower water crossing about 300 meters away from the rest of the unit. When some of the other guys tried looking for him, we couldn't find him.

I have heard the Box Witch likes to tie your boots together and generally fuck with you. One of the older guys told us she'd stand there and stare at you if you're in a truck or knock on the window.

I am also 95% sure some big cat is living in the impact area. I was 200 meters off the northern portion of the impact area, trying to set into a screen line with my truck. While I was ground guiding, I ended up stopping the vehicle and grabbing my dismount to go and check a place where I wanted to set the truck in. We found these big cat-looking tracks in the sand.

Whatever made them must have been big because of how wide and deep they were. Right after that we found some weird shit right (which I'd rather not talk about). My dismount and I looked at each other and were like, "well fuck, I hope we don't get eaten." We "nope'd" the fuck out of there and found a different spot.

Shadows In The box

Yeah, so JRTC. Just last month. So, were a National Guard mounted heavy weapons company. We were doing stand to after dusk as usual, and we had intel that Geronimo was in our AO scouting us.

The night before, we took out some of their guys. So, we were in a defilade watching one of the roads of the intersection we were screening. My driver and dismounts are doing their job of scanning the wood line on our left side, and they see a dude moving in the wood line.

Mind you we're right on the edge of the wood line in camouflage and defilade. My TC looks and sees it too. My dismount and TC pass it up; and get told by PSG to go check it out. They push like 40m into the wood line until they see what we thought was Geronimo.

I'm up on the gun, scanning the wood line with my thermals, and I see no heat signatures. The guys come back and say, "we don't know what he's doing. He's just standing up on the hill." So, my TC and my driver, whose more senior than the dismount, go out again.

Whatever they were seeing was still in the same spot. This time, they used their lasers so I could see where they were looking, and still, I had nothing on my thermals. Then I see them booking it back to the truck just freaked out. When they get back, they're like, "did you see it?" I said no, I saw nothing. They said they were looking at shadow person and suddenly it was gone. None of us in the truck slept that night.

Strange Happenings At The Fort Polk Barracks

Here at Fort Polk, everyone on the floor of my old barracks all had sleep paralysis regularly, out of body experiences while sleeping, and the feeling of being watched once you got on the floor. I had a buddy wake up with scratches—a creepy place all around. I went to check on my Soldiers and got to the floor one day, and immediately felt the urge to run. You know when you were a kid and would pretend a shark was in the pool, and you rush to get out? It's that feeling. I had a known Satanist living here. There was brick outside the building with what appeared to be a goat's foreleg on it. It sat there for months because we were all too spooked to touch it.

106

Here at Polk, I had sleep paralysis pretty frequently in 2018/2019. So much to the point I almost went to Behavioral Health to try and figure it out; but decided not to because that's how people get fucked over. I talked to a friend of mine about it (he lived on the same floor as me and was in my platoon), and he admitted to having the same thing going on ever since he came back from Afghanistan. Not thinking not much of it and thinking it was just a stress thing, I just passed it off.

A few weeks pass, and I meet a mutual friend (who also lived on my floor) who was talking about sleep paralysis. He also said he had it frequently since returning from Afghanistan. Long story short, the more people I met on the same floor as I lived on, the more I learned they all had the same problem. No exception. I wasn't convinced it was something beyond explaining until one night. I woke up to the worst sleep paralysis episode I've ever had.

I had just fallen asleep in my bed when I woke up to my roommate (who lived in the kitchen area of the room) on the other side of the wall making gurgling noises. Spooked, I tried to sit up to go check it out but couldn't. I was trapped and started to panic a little. At the foot of my bed, I had a giant American flag held up by a thumbtack on either corner, and the upper right corner had a cross pin holding it up because I am Christian in faith. The cross pin fell out of the wall, and the flag draped down as if someone had pulled the plug out. That freaked me out.

A few nights pass and I woke up in a cold sweat, not able to move. I squeeze my eyes shut and try to wiggle my toes to start getting out of the sleep paralysis. I faintly hear something whisper my name (my last name, weirdly enough), and I open my eyes, and above me is MY FACE, smiling with no eyes… as if amused I'm stuck.

Sleep paralysis happened so much to us we (almost) became used to it. One night I responded to it with anger instead of fear and never had it since. I moved buildings and refuse to go back to the old floor I used to live on. My experiences weren't isolated. Others got sleep paralysis regularly. The guy directly across the hall avidly believed there were demons up there.

Bog Walker

The Bog Walker is real at JRTC. At first glance, I chalked it up to NVG hallucinations. Longarm figures walking through thigh-deep waters like they are cruising to the 7 Eleven.

Nothing beats the terror that we pass off at the moment. Everyone feels it. But we're all like, "Nah man, that's just G man fucking with us." Seeing is believing in hindsight.

Anybody that knows, knows.

UNITED STATES AIRFORCE

STATESIDE

MIB

My grandfather (who has since passed) had a fascinating life. He was a USAF MAJ in the 50s-60s and was part of, at the time, highly classified proximity nuclear tests in the South Pacific, as well as intelligence stuff with the CIA (mapping, etc.)

He was traveling between bases one weekend, going back to Wright Patterson AFB, when he saw a bright flash. He then woke up 75 miles in the opposite direction in the middle of nowhere with no recollection of how he got there. He always believed in UFOs and extraterrestrials, and given his work, I did and still do believe him 100%.

I have a photo of him somewhere that shows him and his flight crew standing with a nuclear warhead on a runway. The other part is when the space shuttle Columbia exploded over my rural town in east Texas. My dad and I went to town to see all the wreckage. There was a big piece of wing downtown and the state troopers and national guard were standing around. There was a blacked-out Huey there too, with two guys in black fatigues commanding the scene.

I saw a lot of those guys in those few weeks. My dad got them on video. He showed them to grandfather, and he said, "they are the Men in Black." We thought he was joking, but he was dead serious. He said when he worked in the Airforce, he worked with them. He told us they were high level government guys (either NASA or NTSB) that specialized in whatever you would call the Columbia Disaster.

They used quintessential blacked out helicopters, black uniforms, and looked straight out of the conspiracy theory cookbook. A few years later, when my friend and I found a few pieces of the shuttle, we called NASA. They rolled up in blacked out sedans just like the Men In Black. Very cool guys.

Cannon AFB

There was a time when I was stationed at Cannon AFB. I was driving back from my girlfriend's place in Albuquerque and was trying to stay awake by singing to myself. I happened to look up into the sky because sometimes you can see the Milky Way Galaxy out there.

I saw some running lights, and I thought, "that's odd, heavies don't usually fly in formation." That's when I noticed the lights weren't blinking like regular running lights, and also whatever the three dots were, they were covering stars as it passed. Like it noticeably blacked out the sky in a triangle shape.

After that, I stared at the road and sped my way home because I was not about to be abducted. But I just kept thinking that it was large enough to cover stars in the night, but yet there was no sound of engines, no prop sounds, just the sound of the wind on the road.

Edwards AFB - North Base Part I

Regarding Edwards North Base: The north base stuff came about when something happened in the hangar. A phone called the duty desk from that hangar, so dispatch sent patrols and fire. When we got there; the fire department had the truck parked parallel to the front with all the firefighters on the side of the car away from the building.

We said "hey what's going on?" and they said they wouldn't fucking go in there. So, we said whatever we would go in, but we had to wait on the custodian to unlock the doors. The custodian pulled up and said, "Hey, if you guys don't want to go in, I understand," and we were like, why does it matter? The guy responded, "oh, you don't know? That hangar is haunted." We of course said that's bull shit.

Who cares, let's go, but the custodian said, "no, you don't understand. That phone line that called has been cut since the building was in use way back in the old testing days at the north base."

He said people go in (just like we were about to) and look for the phone in an office overlooking the hangar space. You have to go upstairs, and an open hallway wraps around the building to the office. He said people had seen some dark figure inside before. People will go to check the room and the door will be open, and they'll see a figure, which would then sprint at them.

Other times they will walk in, and the door will slam. He said one time, a security forces dude went up into the room and yelled he was going in because the door was open. His partner who was in the hangar heard the door slam and the guy in the room screaming. When the partner looked up to the room window, all he could see a black figure staring at his partner while he screamed in terror.

Eventually the custodian unlocked the door, but he and the firefighters refused to enter the building. The firefighters didn't even want to look at it.

Edwards AFB - North Base Part II

Supposedly in general lodging, a little girl was murdered. Lodging gets calls from the room (where the murder occurred) with no one on the other end. When guests rent the room, they call the desk to complain about the tv switching to cartoons when they are trying to watch something, and a little girl bouncing a ball right outside their room door. People would see a bulge by the dining room table behind the curtain, which was the size of a small child, and then it would disappear.

If the room was empty at night, the room phone would ring relentlessly with no one on the other end. Legally, the front desk must tell people per state law (if they ask about murders in the room) that a little girl was murdered there. So, my dumb ass said give me a room key and went in there one slow patrol to see what would happen.

Nothing abnormal at first. We just sat around waiting. But once we were leaving the back bedroom, the phone started going off. We answered and said very funny to the desk girls. But we received no reply. So we went to put the phone back down, and as we hung up, it started ringing immediately. So, we picked it up, put it down, picked it up a ton of times, and every time the phone instantly started going off.

So, we got the fuck out. As soon as we passed the front door threshold, the phone stopped ringing. I put my foot back inside, and that thing went off. I told all the patrols a few days later, and they all wanted to go.

So, we went back to the room with a fuck ton of people (five or so). Nothing Happened at all, but one guy decided to take some photos while in there. As we are sitting outside on the patrol cars laughing about it, he says, "oh fuck!" Right behind him in one of the photos he took of himself in a mirror in the dining room is a distorted, fucked up looking face that wasn't there when he took the photo.

Goodfellow AFB

I trained at Goodfellow AFB in around June 2007 after DLI, staying in the old motel-style dorms. Two rooms shared a bathroom with Jack and Jill doors, but the sink inside your room is around a corner in the back. The space that shares the bathroom is empty. I had no roommate for a couple of weeks and I was sleeping during the day on the weekend in the single next to the bathroom door.

Woke up to a sound near the sink. A full-on Native American emerges from around the corner. I'm talking loin cloth, feathers, long hair, face paint, and some stick with a gourd rattle on it. He walked toward me, chanting, and lightly shaking the rattle. He got within about three feet of the bed, and I'm shitting bricks. I'm wide awake.

Dude keeps chanting, shaking the rattle, and walks back toward the sink. He stops and turns around, raises the rattle as if to gesture "it's ok," and disappears around the corner. Felt almost protective. After that, the lights in the empty room would turn on and off at odd hours during the day. I'm convinced something else lived in there besides Airmen.

The End Of The Taxiway

I came across a guy that worked as a crew chief at Edwards AFB in the flight test school. One of the test pilots he worked closely with mentioned that he should go to the end of a taxiway on a particular night around 0200. He listened and drove out there. He said it was pitch black, quiet, nothing out there at all…

Then, all of a sudden… this blue sphere of light came shooting across the desert and stopped right over the runway. About 100yds from him. It never made a sound. He said the blue sphere of light was about 5-10ft off the deck and was hovering. Then, without making a noise, it shot back in the direction it came from.

He suspected it came from the direction of Nellis AFB. The next day he saw that pilot on the flight line, and as he was strapping him into a plane, he asked the pilot about what he saw.

When he didn't get a response, he said he asked again. The pilot grabbed the guy by his shirt, pulled him in real close, looked him dead in the eyes, and said, "I don't know what you are talking about." From that point on, the guys went back to prepping for the flight and never said a thing to one another about it.

The Figure In The Briefing Room

I was working at base ops as the SWO (Staff Weather Officer) on a midnight shift. I had just gotten certified to work independently, so it was just the two civilian base ops guys and me. Since it was my first-midnight shift for the week, I did what everyone else did: I stayed up the entire day before. So that when I got off shift at 0800, I'd pass out when I got back to my room.

The first night, I went to fill my water bottle at about 0200. I let base ops know as it meant had to leave the room. I go fill up my water bottle, and about halfway through, I get the feeling I'm being watched. All the hairs are standing up, and I look over to my left.

There's this little nook before the pilot briefing room, and I see a large dark figure standing there. I dismiss it and think I'm just hallucinating since I've been up for over 24 hours. I go back to my desk and tell myself it was nothing.

The next night, at about 0300, I need to fill up my water bottle again. I do the same thing. I watch the pilots briefing room this time. I then see the light in the pilot briefing room go on. I know it's motion-activated, so I tell myself maybe a rat triggered it. Go back to my desk.

Once I get off shift, I test to see how much motion it takes to trigger the lights. I wave my arm in there. Nothing. I step in quickly and then back out. Nope. It took me to go to the middle of the room and do a bit of arm waving to trigger the lights. I was spooked.

Sheppard AFB – "Track!"

So, I attended my technical school at Sheppard AFB and had two instances of seeing things that genuinely freaked me out. The first was when I just barely arrived on base and was running on the mile track near the Tumbleweed DFAC at around 0630 on the weekend. I was the only one out there and had been running for about thirty minutes when I heard a guy say "Track!" right behind me.

This guy, wearing an Air Force PT uniform with a jacket and pants, runs past me. I thought nothing of it and continued my run. After looking down at my phone and switching songs, the guy was gone. As I turned the corner, I felt a cool breeze and got chills all over my body and suddenly felt fatigued. The part that really creeped me out was that I found a PT jacket hanging from a tree at the south end of the track.

Sheppard AFB - Mark

I was from taking classes at the Ground Instruction and Training Aircraft (GITA) ramp. I was on the swing shift, which finished me up around 2300. As my detail was heading back, we'd march back to the dormitories. We'd pass the retired NASA B-52 that had been parked for a few years that the Crew Chiefs would train on.

On a few occasions, my class would see a man in all white who would be working around and servicing the airplane. We asked one of the civilian instructors who had been at Sheppard for several years, and he told us about an instructor named Mark who had been hired from the Dryden Flight Research Center (home of the B-52). Mark had unfortunately died on his drive during his move to Sheppard. According to him, Mark looks after the airplane and keeps things in line since it's been here.

Ellington Field

So I'm from Ellington Field. We had a significant NASA presence during the space program. NASA probably manages close to 60% of our flight line out there.

Some of the buildings used as storage are WW2 vintage, and I've heard talking about how people listen to voices and shit coming out of them now and then.

One of them was so audible that it got the Johnson Space Center (JSC) cops called who opened the building and found absolutely nobody despite several employees hearing banging and voices.

The thought was that somebody got stuck in there and escaped, although it wouldn't surprise me if there weren't other things, especially since the buildings have been around since the 1940s.

Legends Of Edwards AFB

The story of blue eyes was all around the AFRL (Airforce Research Laboratory). There was a lot of talk about haunted shit there (as with most military bases), but everyone knew about blue eyes. The story was that an Airman posted at the gate shack saw the eyes out in the distance.

They darted towards the gate shack, which spooked the Airman, and she shot at it through the gate shack door. The story goes she was then relieved of duty because, you know, she shot at a made-up creature through a door. People would write blue eyes shit all over the buildings out there on the dusty paint, and there was a lot of other creepy shit out there—but none of the blue eye's stories ever mentioned sightings near the main base, just the AFRL.

Another building used to build the X33 (lost funding after 9/11). It was a famous building to explore and see the disassembled spacecraft. One time a few patrols went out there, and one guy stayed behind with the two vehicles. Everyone else went inside and explored. Coworkers say they came out, and he said stuff about "stop messing with me" and "I saw you guys out there," but they were baffled.

So, the consensus is that it was also blue eyes or a creature that looked like a Joshua Tree since the AFRL is littered with them. I don't know if I believe it, but the AFRL was undoubtedly a scary place to be posted alone. Most of the anxiety I'd have or uneasiness was centralized around specific buildings or areas.

There was also a hangar there that had a gym. A K9 handler hung herself there, and the dog wouldn't let anyone near her. So the dog

117

had to put it down to retrieve the body. I'd go work out with other people on shift, but it was terrifying when you'd go alone. You would always feel like something was there, and many windows to other rooms in the hangar were painted over and locked. Very creepy, but it was probably just the vibe.

The tunnels in the AFRL also led to a few weird rooms. The first was the "feeding chamber" that had a single chair bolted to the ground (not sure what it was for, but it was under the NASA test buildings). The whole tunnel system gives off creepy metro vibes, and we were pretty uneasy about the entire thing. Living quarters, offices, and classroom-type areas in "The Morgue." Then a room where the current staff stores different tools and hardware for rocket testing.

There is a bunker complex used for some exercise back in the day. It wasn't a force-on-force thing, but it was seeing if it was feasible for people to live in a bunker or whatever the fuck they were doing back in the day. Everyone called it "The Morgue" because a logbook had the exercises events. Some Senior Airman died in the bunker during the training, although I forget the specific reason. I can confirm that the airman did die; I saw the logbook with my own two eyes when my buddy and I explored the tunnels to see if it was bullshit or not.

OVERSEAS

An Unexpected Hitchhiker

One story my Dad (USAF pilot) likes to tell is the time he was flying MC-130s in some place over Africa, low level, clear night, in full illumination (full moon). He's flying low and looking through NVGs and sees some kind of figure on the ground that looks like its waving at the airplane. Keep in mind he was over the savannah; no major human settlements are around for miles in any direction. He turns around and flies over the figure three times, but on the third time, this figure just vanishes in front of my Dad and his crew. Straight disappears. Everyone in the cockpit saw it.

The real creepy thing is, the two loadmasters in the back kept coming over the intercom like they were talking to someone besides themselves. "Hey man, how did you get in here?" "Where did you come from?" The flight engineer went back to see what was going on, but he found only the two loadmasters.

Both of them were visibly shaken and in shock when they landed; the loadmasters revealed that they saw a dark figure on the ramp (the rear ramp was down, and it was around the time the figure on the ground disappears). When they took off their NVGs to get a better look and turned on the lights, they see this figure of a man who looks like a shadow standing on the end of the ramp. This figure starts walking towards them and then vanishes as soon as the flight engineer came down the cockpit ladder. Needless to say, they were messed up bad after experiencing this. Later, they flew over that same area a few times but never saw anything like it again.

Jumper

Okinawa is the most haunted place the US military is stationed on. One night I was asleep in my barracks room when I heard a blood-curdling scream.

Now, that's not too abnormal for the barracks. Everyone's always up to something. But this was different. It woke me up from my sleep and instantly put me on edge.

This scream sounded like it was a few floors above me. Like someone had opened up their window and screamed into the night. I got up to look outside to make sure we didn't have a jumper.

As I popped my head out the window and looked up, a white form fell right by my face. I looked down to see a body on the ground. I left the window to grab my shoes and get help.

When I got outside, there was no one on the ground. I later learned that a few years before this, a young woman jumped from the roof of our building.

Odo Beach, Okinawa

My buddy and I were exploring this place near Odo Beach in Okinawa. It's on the southern tip of the island. We saw this large cave open to the elements with a central pillar in the middle. There wasn't much to see. We went in on the right side and exited on the left.

As we were leaving, I noticed a small opening into another cave. It was a tight fit, but we thought we could make it through. I led the way, shining my flashlight down the tunnel into this second cave. We were still a bit away from the exit when I noticed that it looked like someone had lived there at one point in time. There were clothes, beddings, and small furniture in this cave.

We decided to leave. We were crawling towards the exit of the tunnel towards this chamber when I heard something scurrying across the cave's floor in front of me.

I shined my light towards the chamber again and saw a small humanoid figure run across the beam. I thought my imagination was getting the better of me, so we kept going. Then it ran across my light beam again, in the direction it first ran from.

I happened to shine my light towards the chamber again. I saw a small, humanoid crouching at the tunnel's exit in front of me. It had long dark hair, bright green eyes, long fingers like claws, and teeth like they were filed to a point. We got the fuck out real quick. We had a friend who wanted to see the cave, so we returned. When we looked for the entrance to this second chamber, it was completely gone, like it never existed.

Kadena Woman In White

I work in logistics. We have a massive set of warehouses on the base where we store packages until the units come to pick them up. I was working nights at the time, and we had a power outage which isn't abnormal. This night it was sweltering, so we decided to open up the warehouse doors to let in a breeze. I went to one end of the warehouse, and my coworker went the other way.

I'd just finished what I was doing and began walking back to our office. I heard some laughing from what sounded like a woman in my coworker's direction, which was weird since we didn't have any women on shift that night.

We had a gym on this side of the warehouses, so I figured it was someone using the gym. I went back to the office, grabbed a flashlight, and cleared out the gym since there was a power outage.

I walked around the corner of the gym to be hit with this cold air, as I'd just walked into a refrigerator. Then I heard the female laughing again and sounded like bare feet on the ground running. I shined my flashlight down the hall and saw something running down the hall—a woman in white with dark hair.

I was going to start to check it out when I heard my coworker calling my name, so I bailed on checking it out. But before I went back to our office, I took one last look down the hall. She was standing there. I bailed immediately. When I got back to the office, I asked my coworker why they called my name. Wasn't him. It turns out he never left the office since we opened the warehouse doors

Grandpa's Stories: Ascension Island

My grandpa was stationed on Ascension Island from the mid-50s to 70s as a radar technician. His military career went from 1949 to the mid-80s.

A big part of his job was monitoring any movement above and on the water in their part of the ocean. The majority of the stuff he would see on the radar was US ships and planes. Since radar tech was in its early days, you had to be good at determining the identity of whatever you saw on screen since most moving objects looked like blobs.

However most military aircraft, boats, and submarines (on the surface) had a very distinctive look to them and very distinctive in how they behaved. You could ID what you're looking at pretty accurately. He would see a lot of soviet ships snooping around and would report them to his supervisor. It was, for the most part, a dull job. A few times were different, though.

He saw a swarm of large objects on the water, moving in a formation compared to a mass of hornets. The things were really big, much bigger than most ships. They were likely spherical. He watched them move across the ocean for a few minutes before the mass moved into a triangular formation, shooting out of the water and into the air. It was bizarre, and when he showed his supervisor, he told him never to talk about it again.

Another time, he saw a spherical object in the sky again, but this time, it was alone. It moved faster than any plane he was used to. Aside from its shape, but the weird thing about it was that it changed direction multiple times, and it did so really erratically. Eventually, it flew off, and his supervisor told him to keep quiet.

He once spotted a huge metal object creeping along the ocean. It was moving steadily and massive in length. He had no idea what it was and couldn't find a reasonable explanation for it when he tried to research what it might be. He assumed it was secret Soviet tech.

Grandpas Stories: Germany

In 1949 my Grandfather was first stationed in Germany. It wasn't that exciting for the most part. He spent most of his time there drinking. Once, he and a bunch of his buddies had some leave time and went off to get smashed in some random German village.

When they got done drinking one night, my grandpa started driving back to the barracks. It was dark, the middle of the night, and they were all smashed, so driving was complicated. Plus, they couldn't remember how to get back. So, my Grandpa was driving pretty bad. He took a turn, and he saw his uncle standing in the middle of the road.

The problem was, his uncle had been dead since WW1. He swerved to miss the apparition of his uncle and ran into a ditch.

The guys he was with cussed him out, and they decided to stay there for the night. I don't know if they had tents or anything. This was four dudes in a jeep.

When they got up the following day and dug the jeep out, they noticed that if my grandpa had kept driving and hadn't swerved, they would have gone right into an old minefield. Uncle's ghost saved his life.

Incirlik Air Base Turkey

Incirlik Air Base Turkey. I was the lone patrol working the night shift in the old munitions' storage area. There have long been stories about a senior SP who killed himself in one of the old Master Surveillance Control Facility Operator (MSCFO) towers and the subsequent hauntings.

I was doing my building checks around 0000 and pulled up to that sector. This place is dark and spooky, and I'm already freaked out. So I'm talking to the guy. "Hey, buddy. Just here to do my job. You know how much it sucks. I'm an Airman just like you," etc., etc.

I've got one eye on the tower and walk up to the first building. As soon as I touch the lock on the door, BAM! All the lights in that sector go out.

I immediately haul ass to the truck, jump in and GTFO. As I looked in the rearview mirror, the only light on was the one in the tower. I drove to the ECP and sat there all night. Pencil whipped all of my checks until the sun came up.

Kadena

While stationed at Kadena, I experienced nothing too crazy myself other than I suspected a ghost in the passenger terminal. The top floor where most of the seating was usually closed at night, but they'd still send someone over there to make sure everything was locked up. As soon as I would get to the stairs without fail, I'd get a really heavy feeling in my stomach.

Like that feeling right before something terrible was going to happen. You could see the windows of the 2nd story from across the flight line, so we'd be out doing a cargo mission late at night, and every once in a while, the lights upstairs would be on when we all knew for sure we turned them off. We'd gotten yelled at a few times by the NCOIC for leaving them on, so we always made sure to check them double.

Overall there was a heavy feeling all over the island. So many people were killed during the battle of Okinawa that it doesn't surprise me it is considered one of the most haunted places in Asia. The Japanese military did some horrendous things to the local population. From talking to the locals we worked with, they would tell up the stories that their grandparents passed down about the torture and rapes that occurred under the Japanese. It's easy to forget that the Japanese military was as bad as the Nazi's if not worse. There are tons of stories and weird happenings there.

AT WAR

Never At Ease

I was a commo guy supporting JTACs when was in Iraq in 2009, near COB Adder. One late night I was driving back to my CLU, I saw a guy in DCUs (which I thought was weird because everyone else was in ABUs and ACUs) rucking it. I thought I would offer him a ride.

I pulled up next to him, looked to my window controls on the left, rolled the passenger window down, and looked back to my right. He was gone. For the rest of the ride home, I avoided looking in my rearview mirror. I know what happens in scary movies.

It didn't hit me till the next day, and I realized that DCUs had been phased out. He had the DCUs on but the BDU pattern battle rattle. I remember in OIF, they had the mix and match.

The "Werewolf Thing"

Nothing super weird, but I'm pretty sure I've seen one of the Afghan werewolf things back in like 2012.

At the time, I was an MQ-9 sensor operator. It was at night, mid-wave IR. We were bringing the aircraft back to base, and I looked around in the valleys.

Something was moving with cat-style mannerisms, but it was the size of a tiger and had a dog-shaped head. It was in the Nangarhar mountains.

Sometimes it isn't easy to assess scale from the sensor when there's nothing around for context, like a doorway or a car. But like I said, based on the terrain, trees, and goat paths, I would say tiger-sized. In midwave IR like that, it was just a black silhouette. I didn't get any details other than the size and shape and how it moved.

Our intel screener thought it may have been a Snow Leopard since we were right on the border with Pakistan, but I'm unsure. We couldn't hang out to look at it, so we just got the one drive-by pass, unfortunately.

From 2010 - 2015, there were so many MQ-9s in the air at any given time, we all saw something weird eventually.

The Quadcopter

The only things I personally saw downrange were dudes taking a piss in the early mornings or taking a shit in the middle of the night. I never saw anything weird, but one of our dudes recorded some pretty weird shit. It didn't make any sense when we saw the recording, and to this day there isn't an explanation for what we saw.

This happened around the first quarter of 2018 in Syria. We always saw these goat farmers in the middle of nowhere. They always had these little huts made of random materials, and they moved every few weeks. This one-night sortie had zero sensor taskings, so the crew decided to watch this random farmer walking around his hut.

These farmers usually had motorcycle, mopeds, or Hilux's. Well, this one farmer hopped onto what looked like his motorcycle. But the weird thing is, he started driving it straight towards his goats! This dude was going reasonably fast, sensors clocked him around 36 mph. Then, all of the sudden, he was "flying" over his goats. The Weapon Systems Officer got about 25 seconds of this farmer on

126

hovering around on some sort of flying motorcycle. We couldn't make any sense of it.

We literally witnessed this farmer flying over his goats on some sort of contraption. Our sniper pods don't have any visual or parallax errors that would produce that. It didn't make any sense.

Our Intel NCOIC thought maybe this farmer jerry-rigged a quadcopter out of a motorcycle. The Intel Shop actually submitted the footage to the Combined Air Operations Center (CAOC) in an actual mission report. The likelihood of a of a random goat farmer having any technology or equipment to pull this off just didn't make sense. The response we got back from the Intel shop was that they had no explanation for what was recorded that night.

"The Kid"

Doing presoak of a town the day before a raid and the sun was almost down. I was scanning around the village, just looking for anything out of the ordinary. All I see are people walking, dogs, cattle, etc. Sun is finally down, and I found some sketchy-looking dudes.

So I'm following them, and they go into this house on the MSR that runs through the village. I see the lights are on inside, so I drop a track and hang out waiting for them to leave. About an hour goes by, and this "kid" shows up. By the looks, had to be between 6 - 9 years old. He walks up and stands in the house's doorway, not moving, staring into the house.

Finally, the kid walks in, and about three seconds later, the lights go out. I think everyone's asleep for the night, so I sit back and start chatting with the pilot, watching the house to make sure nobody else comes or goes. Some time goes by, and I see someone walk out of the house and stand in the doorway. It's the "kid" again.

He's just standing in the doorway looking out into the street and, after about a minute, casually walks away. Because the guys we were following were still in the house, we stayed there instead of following the kid.

Morning comes, and people start crowding around the house. Taking glances into the doorway and then backed up quickly as if they saw something. A big truck rolls up with dudes dressed similarly to the guys who we were following, they hop out, and walk into the house.

They immediately come back out and make everyone back away from the house. One by one, they bring out three bodies. Completely mangled and covered in blood. One looked as if he was missing his arm, the other a leg, and the final looked like his guts had been ripped completely out.

They laid the bodies in the back of the truck and drove away. The only person to show up the entire night to that house besides those three guys was that "kid."

UNITED STATES NAVY

AT SEA

Periscope Depth

I was on a sub as the Officer of the Deck. For whatever reason, my CO kept out three sections on the exact watch leading up to and through our deployment. My section was stuck on the mid-watch, working from 2100 (9:00pm) to 0500 (5:00am) for over a year. We deployed and spent A LOT of time at periscope depth, lights out, in the dark. I'm not talking about a few days. I mean A LOT of time. One of these nights I'm on periscope and I pull my eye off the scope to peek at the sonar, looking for a contact they picked up.

WHOA. I think as I see the CO in the doorway to the sonar, and he is angry. As soon as I focus my gaze at the doorway, he's gone. I chalk it up to me being tired and wired from working so long. So I get back to work.

However, this happens once or twice a night for the next two weeks straight. I start to get irritated and paranoid, so I bring it up to my Diving Officer of the Watch and Radio Division Chief. They both say something along the lines of "Oh, THAT guy."

It turns out they and many other crewmembers have seen this guy too, out of the corner of their eyes, standing in the doorway glaring at them. They told me, "we don't look at him anymore, just ignore him."

It relieved me to know I wasn't crazy, but I was not comforted by the fact we were all seeing the same guy—an angry man in a navy boiler suit. I never could figure out who it was. But we all would stop seeing him when we left our mission areas. But as soon as we went back out to our mission areas and went to periscope depth… he always came back.

Sea Stories Part I

My friend and I (both flight deck night check) have experienced some creepy shit during a three-month patrol we were on.

We were walking back from getting snacks from the vending machine, going back upstairs to the deck to watch some anime with the projector. We are walking in lit space, no red lights or anything. Suddenly, the hatch in front of us (that I'm about to grab) just suddenly dogs open and swings open about five feet from us.

We both step to the side to let another person through (only to see that after a few seconds) no one was there. I thought I was tripping, so I was like, "bro, did I open that hatch." and he responds, "Nah, there should be someone on the other side or something." We both checked, but there was no one there.

It's 0200 down in the bottom of the ship, and this door flies right the fuck open in front of us. I looked around to see if it was just some wind or something. Nope. Nothing. It freaked us both the fuck out. Our supervisor didn't believe anything we had to say and said we just made it up trying to be funny or something.

Sea Stories Part II

One night, when we were literally in the middle of the ocean, we had to darken the lights on the ship for some reason. There was no lighting on the flight deck. Every two hours, we roved around the deck to see if anyone was up there at night when they shouldn't be.

We had all the weight stacked up forward. While up forward, you could hear the wind scraping against the birds (aircraft), making whirling sounds and whatnot, and that itself is kind of creepy when you're walking around with just flashlights.

Back aft was completely clear. No aircraft. Walking around aft without a flashlight was like staring into a blank void with nothing there. But when we walked back aft, we both heard voices and a faint rotor sound. I checked the external catwalks that run along with the ship. No one. My buddy checked the other side, no one. We got the hell out of there and went back inside right after that.

Sea Stories Part III

The Pway on the 02 deck. It runs throughout the ship and such. You can see down it. I was walking through it at night when I heard hatches opening and creaking. Didn't think anything of it at all.

Red lights are on, and when I look through the porthole on the door that is far away, it looks pitch black through it. But then I got closer, and it deadass looked like someone was staring through it.

WHEN I TELL YOU I STOPPED DEAD IN MY FUCKING TRACKS. I must have looked like a deer in the headlights. I was moving my head around to see if this person or whatever was going to move, but they just stared motionless at me. After about ten seconds of no movement, I ran right the fuck back upstairs. No thanks dog, I'd rather not.

SNOOPIE Team

On my first deployment, I was part of a team called the SNOOPIE Team. We were there to take pictures of vessels for intelligence purposes (i.e., hull number, the flag being flown, engine tacks, etc.). This is basically to make sure ships we are seeing aren't spoofing us and are using the correct names. It was a counter drug operation deployment, so there are a lot of boats that did this.

I was sleeping in my rack one night, and over our ship announcement system, I hear, "AWAY SNOOPIE TEAM AWAY, PORT SIDE." I am dazed because they quite rarely make announcements during "normal" sleeping hours unless it's an emergency. Once I realize it, I rush to get ready, head to my space and grab the camera then run to the bridge (it was a small navy ship, so I was able to do all this in about a couple of minutes).

When I get up there, everyone that is on watch and isn't steering the ship is on the bridge wing staring up into the sky (Including our CO, which made this even weirder). There is this glowing green thing in the sky darting around unlike anything I had ever seen or heard of.

I take some pictures, we all "ooh and aww" at it for a while, and then it is just gone. The ship CO told me to save the pictures to the laptop we had just in case, and then it just never got brought up again. I couldn't keep them to a personal laptop or anything (because you can't do that), so I have no proof. But every once in a while, I think about it how genuinely bizarre it was.

USS Monterey

My ship had a contractor die during ship construction in RADAR 1. The guy was crushed between the forward SPY radar array and the bulkhead. In general, RADAR 1 and the 03 levels have some spooky things going on. Such as footsteps when there's no one there, valves closing for no reason, and if you go in the space and try to talk to this contractor, he will slam the door shut or something like that.

In Key West for a port visit, I think it was about January 2011. The hatch to get on the IFF platform had broken hinges, so once opened from below when standing on the ladder, it just fell onto the platform. The platform had antennas going around the outer edge in a big circle, and the hole you climbed through (the hatch covered that) was how to climb up onto the platform.

We were up there a few hours taking measurements and decided to break for lunch. We left everything up there because we were coming back after lunch. Tools, cables, and the hatch laying open out on the deck. While eating up in our shop (just down the passageway from the bottom of the mast where we were working), this chief comes running in screaming about how he was just nearly killed because of our negligence.

It turns out that hatch, which weighed at least 20 lbs, had somehow fallen from the IFF platform down to the 03 levels, missing the chief by only a couple of feet. We couldn't believe it! No one was up there, and it couldn't have moved on its own.

The hole it covered had a 2-inch lip where it rose 2 inches above the deck, so that it couldn't have slid and fallen through. The outer edge of the platform had antennas that came up about 10 inches above the deck, and there was no space between the deck and the antennas.

No explanation for how it could have fallen. That chief was a total asshole, constantly screaming at his division, getting in their faces and cursing so loud we could hear it down the way. I believe that ghost from RADAR 1 tried to kill him for being such a piece of shit by throwing the hatch down at him.

The Weird Space

My first ship was an old Frigate. I'm not one to believe in the supernatural usually and I genuinely think there is an answer for everything, but on my ship was a space where weird shit just seemed to happen.

Things would go missing or be moved into weird spots. We were underway, and it was late at night, and I was in the space alone. Now it was the lowest and most forward space of the ship, one of the SONAR spaces. NO ONE outside of other sonar men ever came up that far and didn't at 0300. It was way out of the way and was a hike to get to.

Sitting there listening to music and reading, I hear a monster banging on the space hatch, like someone whacking it with a wrench or something. It scared the absolute shit out of me. I hop up, mad as fuck, and race over to the door. I swing it open, and no one is there.

Directly across from the door was a ladder well that went up to the next deck, and I heard boots walking on the balcony above. Before I can move, I listen to a voice trailing off saying: "Chief needs you in Sonar." But I do not recognize the voice. It doesn't sound like anyone in the division.

I climb up, see no one around. Confused, I decided I would walk to SONAR. On my trip there, I didn't encounter anyone until I got into Sonar Control. I encountered the dude who has been on watch for a considerable amount of time. He tells me no one has been to that space or looking for me, definitely not our chief.

Part of me thinks it had to be someone fucking with me, but it

134

creeped me out enough I limited my time alone down there at night. It bothers me that years and years later, no one still has admitted to it despite our meetups and reminiscing about the old days and pranks we pulled.

USS Barry

This was on USS Barry (DDG 52). I will stand by this story till the day I die. Easily ten other people saw this, and so did multiple radars.

There I was, and this is no shit. Middle of the Atlantic Ocean, and absolutely nothing was going on. It was a super calm night, no waves, no moon, no land for a thousand miles, we are all alone. We were trying to stay awake on the bridge, talking about nothing, when suddenly a bright mini sunrise happened on the horizon.

As soon as we saw this light, the air search radar guys called up to see if we could see an object in the sky. Sure enough, our eyes and the sensors saw the same thing. Almost instantly, this object moved directly above the ship.

As we watched this happen, the radar guys came running to the bridge. They had seen the object move on radar and wanted to see it. I am freaked out by now and call the captain. He doesn't seem to care. We all stand out on the bridge wing and watch this... thing... hover there at 10's of thousands of feet.

After about 20 minutes, it disappeared, just gone. As rapidly as it had moved from the horizon to above us, it simply shrank from sight.

USS Frank Cable

I am a CIVMAR (civilian) sailing with US Navy's Military Sealift Command (MSC). I was on the USS Frank Cable. There is a pump room called "pump room one" at the bottom of a 45-foot ladder. It's the bottom of the ship.

When you have watch, you have to make rounds, and one of the stops was down in that pump room, so anytime you had the 0000-0400 or the 0000-0600 watch, you had to go down there in the middle of the night.

Often, you would look down and see someone stepping off the ladder and going into the pump room. But when you got down there, nobody would be there. It was weird the first few times, but eventually, I got used to it.

It was always super creepy down there, like you wanted to get in and out as fast as possible. Everyone who stood that watch had seen the same thing too: a person stepping off and walking away into the empty room.

USS Ronald Reagan

USS Ronald Reagan, it was on the 22-02 watch, and it was a pitch-black, moonless night crossing the Bermuda Triangle.

We lost the primary gyrocompass, then GPS for a while, and the ICs were reporting weirdness happening in Aft IC with the backup (I was hanging out in Central as the 1 Plant PE on a proficiency watch).

It was probably about an hour that we were without the compass, just plowing ahead on a straight-line path trying to find some stars to verify where we were. There were no visible stars in the night sky! Suddenly everything came back up, the stars were visible again, and we could confirm our position was exactly where we thought we were.

After I got off watch a bit later, I ran into a couple of buddies of mine on the smoke pad also next getting off watch. One of them had been on the bridge, and the other one had been a lookout aft on the catwalks.

They both claimed that several topside watches had reported hearing mysterious voices, sounds of chains dragging, and a bell ringing. So much so that one terrified lookout had repeatedly begged to be relieved. This all happened while we were blind and lost indications.

"Did you see that?"

When my ship was in the yards (USS Boxer), I spent about a year on our corrosion prevention team. We had a job come in that involved us doing repairs to a supply shop three decks down.

One of our guys volunteered to go down to the space to assess damage (note: there was no working lighting in there, so he had to use his cell phone flashlight). Within a few minutes, he sprinted back up to our office, heaving and looking terrified.

He said that while down there, he heard a noise behind him, and when he pointed his light toward the sound, he saw a heavy-duty light cover get pushed off of a table and shatter everywhere.

Not knowing him to be a liar but being somewhat skeptical, I wasn't sure what to think. So another one of the guys and I went to see for ourselves since the first dude refused to go back down there.

When we got down there, it looked creepy. In place of a door was a cheap piece of board, and the space itself was like a long, dark hallway leading to another, adjacent pitch-black and even creepier hallway.

We find where the light cover shattered, and there are two more intact on the same table. These things weighed maybe 10 pounds, so there was no way it just rolled off, and the whole thing felt uneasy. We kept trudging on and assessing the damage to the deck.

Now, to the part that freaked me out: we walked over to the barely-lit entrance and stood there for a minute or two to converse before leaving, with my partner facing the light just outside and me facing away. While he's talking, an opaque shadow crosses over his face. He stops mid-sentence, and his gaze slowly moves over my head, clearly spooked. He asked, "did you see that?" I said, "yeah."

Judging by the shadow, something translucent had to have walked behind me because no solid object could've done what we saw. Plus he clearly would've seen someone walk by the entrance, and I would've heard it. The weirdest thing I've seen since I've been in.

The Void

I was a Steam MM aboard the USS Bonhomme Richard. We had been working nonstop because the previous Chief left the ship in a mess. We got to repairing the void spaces for cracks, and I'm on balls (0000) watch one day—no one in the space but me.

I'm making my rounds. Listening for if something is breaking because everything is constantly breaking. I see a boot pull into the open void space. I get confused and run towards the space and hear a loud crash. The tarp was we had left to cover the entrance was still tied down over it with caution tape.

I peeled it back, and no one was there. Heard from the ship old-salt that some inspector fell down that same void and snapped his neck in the 70s.

"Well, I guess I gotta go."

Having 48–96-hour workdays were pretty standard for E4+ USS Bonhomme Richard. I was on TGUL (turbine-generator upper level) watch for the first time. I'm leaning on a handrail after rounds. Some guy walks by talking to me, but I don't hear him because I'm tired and in a daze.

He sits down on the rail next to me and starts talking for a few minutes. Again, I am in a daze and I am not listening to him. But then I catch him say, "Well, I guess I gotta go." He turns right and walks straight through the bulkhead. Only after the shock wore off did I realize he was wearing dungarees, the type of uniform worn when this very ship was commissioned during the Vietnam War.

Ghosts Of The Bonhomme Richard

One time we were mustered and had all hands-on deck search party to try to find a man seen by contractors in the engineering areas while in the yards. When the engineers were told who they were looking for, laughing and shrugging they said, "he's always been around."

Once I was chilling down in main issue and had a shadow figure rush down one ladder well, run past me, and into the engineering space on the other side of the room. When it ran past me, it knocked paper on the floor.

There was a young daughter of a khaki who died after she fell down the ladder well by the elevator in the mess decks. She likes to play a music box and bounce balls up and down the p-ways. I've personally seen her late at night on my rounds.

The funny thing is after the fire I was placed on the duty section. One guy went up on the ship to do his rounds and he came rushing back because he heard a music box playing by the COs office. Man, that was a fun watch that night.

Last watch I had before we shut her (the ship) up: I was walking with my partner and we went past the mess decks. Over there we heard the little one humming and walking up the ladder well. I know it was her because no one else was on besides us and we controlled the only access point.

Sounding Security

On my first ship, I was sounding security on the 0200-0700. Around 0300, we get a call from central while pumping down FWD to go pump down AFT. Our shitters were a big issue on deployment.

Anyways I needed to use the head and my berthing was on 2nd deck, so I just had to go up one deck. I told my qualified watch I would meet him at shaft alley (since that's where he was going). On my walk to shaft alley, I hit the mess line, and medical is right there. I look up and I see someone walk out of medical. I didn't hear the door or see the light, but I saw it was someone walking with a limp. I thought, "oh, I'll see who it is when they hit the log room." Because we always kept the lights on in the log room.

As soon as they hit the log room, I got chills. They had on what looked like green coveralls and a green foul weather jacket, and they were carrying what looked like a mask.

I started to speed up because I was like, "what the fuck" and wanted to see who was being creepy at 3 am. I'm not even two seconds behind this person, and they took a right-back by shaft alleys p-way. They just disappeared. There were a few places they could have gone. From where I was standing, you would be able to see everywhere they could have gone. I wasn't the only one to see something like this.

Gulf Of Alaska

So, I've had a couple of weird experiences during my four years but only one that I cannot explain. This was in early may in the Gulf of Alaska on the flight deck. Setting the scene: it is cold, windy (about a good 30 mph), and off and on raining. It's about 0200 or so, which in Alaska at this time of year is only a few hours after sunset and a few before dawn. It's cloudy - meaning there's no moon out, and it's pitch black. This is important.

I can't remember who pointed it out first, but at least three of my guys and I saw it. Roughly a mile off the starboard side was a beam of light running more or less parallel to the ship. From what I could see, it was about a mile long. My first thought was that it looked like a spotlight along the surface, but we had no aircraft in the sky, we were the only ship insight, and it was not coming from our ship. It got weirder when in the center of this beam of light, a very bright circle of light appeared.

This looked like another spotlight but just under the water's surface and pointing straight upwards. This narrow beam moved laterally along the horizontal shaft a little bit, before returning to the center and slowly getting dimmer and dimmer. Eventually, I had to get back to work, but I watched this for maybe seven minutes.

If you're thinking "submarine," I've seen subs doing their thing. This was not a sub. I'm not sure if this was something I wasn't supposed to see or not, because I've had a couple of those experiences (none of those I can share unfortunately). That's it. I wish it were longer, but that memory lives rent-free in my mind.

On another carrier (not the same one I saw the lights on), I saw a hatch open in front of me with nobody on the other side. I don't know if you've been on a ship before, but hatches don't just open from drafts. Usually, they take upwards of at least ten pounds of force to open. But there was nobody there to open the hatch.

USS Denver

The number three generator room on the USS Denver is haunted. I was on machinery watch in port making rounds and taking readings. I got to the generator room, opened the hatch, closed the door, slid down the ladder, and started taking the readings. There were two doors in the gen room, one forward, one aft, and the upper level was all open grating.

I heard footsteps walk across above me. When I called out, no one answered. I couldn't see anyone. I went up the ladder and looked around, but no one was in the compartment with me. After that, I would open the door, slide down the ladder, look at the gauges, and get the fuck out. Only after closing the door behind me, I'd enter the info in my logs.

The story was that a GMG used to hang out with the engineer in charge of the generator (Vietnam era), and they'd smoke pot. The GM was doing maintenance on the aft gun and somehow triggered a loading cycle while he was in it. It proceeded to load a good portion of the GM into the weapon. The story was that his ghost was hanging around in the Generator room.

All I know is I heard the boots cross the grating (you can't mistake that sound), and there was no one in the compartment with me. Whatever it was, I avoided that room as much as I could. Unfortunately for me: my GQ station was the No. 3 switchboard immediately aft of the generator room, but I would take the long way to get to it rather than go through it.

USS Iwo Jima

I was in the USS Iwo Jima. I have always suffered from sleep paralysis. But on this particular cruise, I kept having a weird recurring dream about a nun without a face trying to kill me.

The day after, I went on ship tax, and I met a dude named Murph.

Murph and I became friends quickly, and we both talked about our "gifts," how I could see spirits in the forms of auras and how he could see them as "transparent people" and even speak to them.

A few days passed, and my buddy told me he went to the upper v of the ship and played the Ouija board because he wanted to contact this presence we all felt in the boat. A few days later, he passed out on the smoke deck. I think he contacted this thing and identified it as a demon. As the days followed: the presence got stronger, my sleep paralysis got more frequent, and more weird shit started happening.

Things were getting thrown off the kitchen shelves. I wanted to put that on the ship rocking until I saw a black hand come through the wall and knock things over. Murph and I heard both our first names being called by a female voice. There were endless stories among the of a "little girl" who would run around at midnight. I saw her maybe two times running around while I was on duty. But she never bothered me.

Red Sea Lookout

I'm pretty sure this was on my first deployment in 2006. We were in the Red Sea. I had only been on the ship for about three or four months at this point. I was still getting used to the fact that the ocean has algae that sort of glows when it is disturbed. So, you can see aquatic life swimming around as it disturbs the water. For example, dolphins look like torpedoes coming in. That's pretty terrifying the first time you see that especially on deployment.

I was on a forward lookout reporting any ships, aircraft, or debris that I can see. Sometimes there's not a lot to report. You spend a lot of time looking at the water. It was a decently warm night, and we were transiting at probably 15-20 knots to wherever we were going at that time. I noticed a pretty good-sized light spot in the water, probably two or three hundred yards off to the side of the ship. It looked similar to a school of fish in the water to me at first. It was round in shape. Not bright, like there was something with lights on under the water.

I didn't think much of it. But what threw me off about it was that it was coming towards the ship and matching our speed. I thought these are some swift fish. So, I reported it to the Officer of the Deck and he blew me off at first. I'm sure he thought the same thing I thought initially.

But it never changed shape. It stayed perfectly round, and it stayed right next to the ship about 100 yards out. After about 10 minutes of me telling him that I don't think this is a school of fish, he came out and looked. It then moved under the ship.

We both followed it to the other bridge wing, and it stayed on that side of the ship about 100 yards away for a few minutes. He didn't think it was a school of fish anymore either, but neither of us had any explanation of what it could be. It then began to move from one side of the ship to the other; staying even with the ship and matching our speed. It never changed shape for the hour it was with us before it drifted off. I was on that ship for about three years, and I never saw anything like that again.

Any aquatic life leaves a water disturbance trail behind it. This thing left no path, and it was perfectly round the whole time. I've also never seen a whale keep up with a ship. Dolphins yes. But they legitimately look like torpedoes in the water.

ASHORE

English Hall

I believe in the paranormal, but I never thought I'd encounter it. I've stood three mid watches at English Hall, and I distinctly remember them because of what I encountered.

My first mid-watch was about 0100 in the morning, and like the shit bag I am, I was bull shitting with the POOD when we heard footsteps coming from the stairwell adjacent to the door. I turned to the POOD and asked if there was still anyone in the building (we were required to log everyone entering and exiting the building after 2100). He said the last person checked out at around 2230.

Being all "Joe Navy," I figured I'd investigate and "catch" this person who didn't sign into the logs. I started up the stairs and got up the first landing to where I could see down the hall of the 2nd floor. This is the point where things get weird. I started to feel cold, like irregularly cold, and felt this unshakeable feeling of not being in the right place. I felt as if I wasn't supposed to be there. The feeling, to this day, I can't fully explain.

Well, I continued. As I continued the footsteps grew louder, so much so that I fully expected that I would be face to face with the person who didn't sign into the logs. But when I rounded the corner, the hair on my neck shot straight up. There was no one there. I nearly pissed myself and ran down the stairs. The POOD didn't believe a word of my story, nor would I have my following two mid-watches been normal.

The next mid-watch I stood in English Hall was a few weeks later. The CPO lounge was on the second floor, and the door to it was required to be shut, not locked but shut according to my logs. As I walked down the hall doing my rounds, I noticed the lounge door was fully open. So, I approached and looked inside through the door jam, the lights were off in the room and it appeared to be empty.

144

I decided to close the door and continue my rounds. I reached for the doorknob. Right before I broke the plane of the door jam, the door slammed shut in my face. Again, I nearly pissed myself and ran. I told the POOD everything. Again, the building was empty.

Finally, my last mid-watch I stood in English Hall. I'm doing my rounds of the basement. There's a door at the end of the hall that I was supposed to check to be SHUT and LOCKED per my logs. As I approached the door, I was about halfway down the aisle when suddenly that feeling of cold, not belonging, not alone, came to me. There was a red light above the door, and I noticed it flickering.

As unsettling as it was, I continued, but the light went out. I figured the light must have burnt out, but then the fluorescent light nearest to the door started flickering...and then it went out, and then the next, and the next, gradually getting closer to where I was standing. I ran. Not walk fast, I fucking ran. I never did another round down there again. The fear was so intense. I have never been so scared in my life. I heard from a few nubs that English got shut down a little while back, and I say good. Fuck that place.

Shipmates

I was part of the crew of the SECOND SHIP that had collisions at sea in Singapore, where 10 of my shipmates perished in their sleep. We were docked in Changgi, and we turned the messdecks into more of a lounge since food service stopped on the ship and we get food deliveries. We had Igloo Jugs with water or tea for some refreshments while doing ship work throughout the day. One of my GM1s had a midwatch, so he went to the mess decks to grab a coffee.

He realized there was another sailor across the mess by the jugs. His movements looked like he was getting water and drinking it. Then he walked casually out the other door with his back turned without saying anything, so my GM1 didn't see who it was. Being in the ship, we have a few common gestures to each other when we realize someone else is in the same space. We look at each other and say "Hey!" or nod to acknowledge each other's presence. This struck him as odd, but it was almost 0000, so he wasn't really in the greeting mood.

Then it hit him - the slick backed hair, 6'4" figure, and sleeve tattoo could NEVER be mistaken for anyone else but one of the sailors that died a few weeks before and still currently interred within berthing (it took a while to get the bodies out because the water inside the berthing where people drowned was holding the weight on that part of the ship). My GM1 is a quiet and straightforward guy and not keen to joke about something like that, especially when it's related to the collision.

Another story: when the chaos happened during the collision, the whole crew is running around to get to their respective repair lockers. One of my shipmates accounted for one of his friends during muster because he RAN into him. My shipmate was wearing firefighting gear and helmet in the dark, so he only got a good look at the name tag of the person. But the person told him, "Please do a good job of saving everyone else!" in the familiar voice of his friend, then moved out of sight around a corner. My shipmate could never explain or grasp it when he found out his friend, who he knows he saw, never made it out of berthing alive.

Yokosuka Japan

MWR did a retreat program for our crew to Tama Hills Resort in Yokosuka, Japan. The resort was an old Japanese ammo depot turned into a retreat resort where they built cottages, a paintball ground, a horse range, and other kinds of relaxing activities. We were given a key to multiple golf carts to explore the base.

My SH1 and I were riding off into the afternoon just before sunset. It was winter, cold but no snow or fog, clear as day but it was getting dark. I was driving, and as soon as we came up this line of trees, he asked me to stop. He took a picture of the road ahead, which I thought was a nice view. He then was quiet, and I kept driving when we passed old ammo barracks.

The shutters and doors were rotted away, so I drove through and out of these barracks. He wasn't excited and just stayed quiet. I thought, maybe he wasn't thrilled, or I was too much. We headed back to the hotel. During dinner, he showed me the picture he had taken. As clear as day, and out of place, was a dark figure. You can only see half of his body, waist down. The figure's legs looked like

146

he was in a marching pace, where you exaggerate your steps, forward legs straight out. It made me instantly weak because the direction is towards the ammo barracks.

Another story: when we got to Tama Hills, I got assigned to one of the cottages with a buddy. He hung out with some people, so I was alone, and I decided to take a shower. I put on Spotify on my phone and set it down on the dining table by the head. I already had an eerie feeling as soon as I walked in, like I wasn't alone. So I blasted music to distract me, bathroom door open. Halfway through the shower, the music stopped, and I heard someone walking in straight to one of the rooms. It was a wooden cottage so that you could clearly hear footsteps.

Less than five minutes go by, I dried off, and (you guessed it) no one was there but me. What's also weird is when I grabbed my phone, Spotify was still playing, only the volume was turned down. I didn't unload my things, so I got dressed quickly. I could feel my stomach coming up my throat and feeling closed in, and I went to my friends staying at the actual hotel.

Not surprised to find out later that evening that most of us stayed at the hotel, like eight people in one room, some sleeping on the floor. Because the cottages made them uneasy and felt like they were being watched.

Echoes Of The Rising Sun

I was SDO one week, closing down after the day around 1800 or so. I was finishing locking down the Chief's Mess when I heard shouting out beyond our parking lot. I walked out the main gate, through the parking lot, and onto the road. It almost sounded like cadence.

I figure it must be EOD doing night ops or something, but I still don't see anybody. I wander down the mountain road to the main access road and I see a regiment of Soldiers marching down the road.

They were Imperial Japanese Army Soldiers! They were carrying arms of the day (I distinctly remember the Arisaka because I'm a gun nut) at parade arms, just marching on by as if they were headed to a new position. I didn't say anything, I just stood there and watched. After a minute, the last man had passed.

I gave it a few seconds before I walked down to Main Access, but there was no one in the direction they were headed. It didn't faze me much since this wasn't the first ghostly encounter I've had, but it was odd nonetheless.

Scratching At The Door

I was in FC-A School in 1999, at the brand new (at the time) barracks. These barracks are so brand new that the five beds in my room still had plastic wrap on the mattresses, and I was the first person to be in the room.

It's the weekend, and it's late (or maybe early morning). I was playing some OG PlayStation at the time since the Xbox and GameCube hadn't even been released yet. I'm just chilling and playing either Final Fantasy VII or Tactics. I am the only person in the room, and I still have no roommates yet.

I hear something scratching around in the room, I try to ignore it at first. I stop playing and listened. There it is again. I decide to follow the sound. It ends up leading me to my closet. I stop outside my closet and listen. Something is definitely inside my closet and scratching at the door.

So as a young and dumb 19-year-old kid...I open the door.

There is nothing there. Just my uniforms and civvies hanging up and my two empty seabags folded on the floor. When I close my closet, I notice there are scratches on the door, about a foot and a half to two feet above the bottom of the door. I look around the closet, and there are no holes in the wall one would associate with rodents, no vents, or anything where a giant rat (and to leave claw marks 18" to 24" upon the door it would have been a BIG rat) could have darted to when I opened the door.

I closed the door, and then I hear scratching again. Now its outside the window by my desk where my crappy TV from the NEX and my PlayStation is. If my room had been on the ground floor, this wouldn't have irked me. But my room was on the 2nd or 3rd floor of the barracks. Maybe the 4th floor. I forget how big the barracks were, but there was no way I was on the ground floor.

I don't even look at this point. I throw on some coveralls, straight run out of my room and out of the barracks. I find my room and look up… nothing there. I went to the office where the shore duty guys who ran the barracks did their work and told them what happened.

They thought I was crazy. A few of them, including a Chief, went to my room, and I showed them the scratch marks in my closet. When it was light out, they looked at my window from outside and noticed more scratch marks outside my window.

Everyone was as confused as me. My first roommate arrived that week, and I never heard it again. They did replace my closet door before I left, though.

Kadena Air Base

2016 at Kadena Air Base, Okinawa, Japan. Just down the Flightline a bit from the old TOC building, we were testing some SATCOM gear in an old hangar. While my buddy was doing his thing, I got bored and walked around the hangar.

There were a few lights on, so I turned them all off. I came back down to check on my buddy. I turned around and looked up at the offices I was just in, and the lights were back on. WHAT THE FUCK.

Scotland

2018 at Mansefield hotel, Elgin, Scotland. I was there on deployment (no shit), in a two-room cottage-style place set away from the rest of the hotel. I heard my upstairs roommate walking up his stairs and walking around upstairs after we all got back from somewhere.

I happen to look out the window, and there he is talking to someone about 30 feet away from the cottage. I called out to him, saying what I heard upstairs. We ran up to his room, opened the door, only to find no one inside. Prior to this, his room had motion-sensing lights that would always come on around 0200-0300 in the morning and wake him up. He didn't stay there much longer after this.

Camp Lejeune Hospital

I am a Navy Nurse and this took place in 1994 at NH Camp Lejeune, the NEW hospital. There is an old hospital on base that was known to be haunted, but it was mostly closed up when I was there. This story applies to the new hospital. Ward Three East, if you're familiar with it.

This was my first duty station out of A School. The ward was run by civilian RN's and HM's. There were locker rooms down the hall going towards the other ward, Ward Three West (vacant and unused).

The two wards were back-to-back with each other. It wasn't a long walk, but it took a few minutes to get to the locker room. One side of the hall was glass that looked out over the parking lot during the day. During the night, the glass acted like a mirror.

There was a civilian RN who was a true workaholic, who always wore this type of distinct blue scrubs, and she was well-loved by the staff because she was always willing to stay late or do whatever needed to be done. She also wore a specific scent of perfume so that you could smell her coming.

One night (before my time), she stayed too late, fell asleep going home, crashed her car and died on impact. Her ghost was said to haunt the halls of Three East, particularly around the locker room and that glassed-in hall area.

One night I was headed down to the locker room and was utterly alone, not another staff member in sight and no patients on that side. Suddenly I smelled perfume. At this point, I had no idea perfume was part of the haunting or that it was hers.

I just went to the bathroom and was overwhelmed by the smell of it. Walking back down that glass hallway, I looked in the glass. In the reflection was a woman walking behind me in blue scrubs, wearing her stethoscope, and various nursing stuff hanging off of her

150

uniform. I take about ten steps or so, turn to see who it was, and say something… but the hall was empty. After a pause, I kept walking, and heard footsteps follow me back to the nurses' station.

I had heard rumors of a ghost, but no one was willing to tell me if the story was true. Later that night when I told the other nurses about the woman I saw and about the perfume in the air, that convinced the other nurses to tell me her story.

"Pardon"

When I was at Pearl Harbor for the 2018 RIMPAC, I was TAD with the USS Carl Vinson. We were there for 12 days, just chilling and partying. I can't remember why but we couldn't do laundry on the ship and had to use the base laundromat. You could take a bus there, but it was quicker to walk back because of the wacky bus schedule/route.

I was on my way back from the laundromat one night. I walked with some headphones in around 2300 back to the pier: about a mile or mile and a half. I was walking on the sidewalk on my way back, when I got the feeling I had just stepped into a walk-in freezer, which is weird as hell in Hawaii during July of all places.

I didn't stop walking but I paused my song at apparently the perfect moment, because I heard going past me, clear as day, a "Pardon me." It was spoken in a perfect southern accent, and sounded very close to me. There was no one around but me, and I was the only one out there that night. I wouldn't say it freaked me out, but I hurried back to the ship after that and quickly back to my rack

NAS Leemore

I was stationed with VA-97 out of NAS Lemoore in the 1980s through the '90s. Now NAS Lemoore was where all the A-7 attack aircraft were assigned on the West Coast, so we did not have any fighter aircraft assigned to this base. In December 1991, I was on a line watch. The time was about 2300. Our hangar and flight line faced west towards Coalinga and the San Benito Mountain.

I was making my rounds checking the aircraft on the flight line when I saw two F-14 Tomcats taxing out to the west runway. I thought it odd being this late and on a Saturday night; but put it off as a couple of cross-country birds doing a sortie that had stopped for fuel. As soon as they turned onto the end of the runway, they immediately went full afterburner. They were pointed south on the runway and once they lifted off, they immediately backed hard to the west and climbed.

I watched as they leveled out, then about five seconds later, I saw a missile launch from the lead Tomcat. I watched the missile track north over the San Benito Mountain and disappeared behind a cloud. I heard this pop sound and witnessed a bright, fluorescent green light that was at least a 1/2 mile across illuminate the sky. The color was like a glow stick, and it looked as if it had a stained the cloud it was behind. This light hung in the sky for at least 15 minutes and then just dissipated into the night sky. I radioed it in to my Hangar OOD and told him what was going on. He said he'd call it in.

I was called into my XO's office the following Monday and asked what took place on my watch. I told him what had happened and then I was dismissed. I never heard anything about it afterward. I don't know what it was, but I believe we engaged something that wasn't anything of ours. It was just the way everything happened, and never hearing anything about it just gave me the strangest feeling about it.

USS Baitfish
Museum Volunteer

I was staying on the USS Baitfish (WWII sub) while volunteering to assist with the restoration. I slept overnight on the sub with another volunteer (an old man). Every night I'd wake up to loud, heavy, cranking noise coming from the engine room next to the enlisted sleeping quarters. Around that same time, I'd hear the distinct sound of pans moving in the galley. This freaked me out because, firstly, the engine room is empty of tools, and the engines are seized. Secondly, the kitchen has pots and pans for display during tours, but they were quite literally locked in a cabinet.

I didn't want to check, so I went back to sleep after both noises stopped. In the morning I found rusted tools that looked like they had been lost at some point, littered about the engine room. They were no longer usable, that's how rusted they were. The engine cylinders also look like they moved overnight. I remembered the cylinders were not at the top of their cycle. Which made no sense to me, because (even with help) there was no way I could get those cylinders to move.

Then I went into the kitchen. The pots and pans are scattered across the kitchen. Keep in mind there are only two of us on the boat and the old guy took sleeping pills. Neither of us had access to the key for the galley either. We put everything back the best we could, put the tools in the museum building, and locked the pots and pans up with a new lock.

The next night, the same thing happened again. But this time it was louder, like whatever was making the noises didn't give a fuck anymore about being quiet. I heard grunting and tools clanging coming from the engine room, and the sound of pots and pans getting thrown all over the galley. In the morning, the pots and pans were inexplicably back out and the new lock missing.

The engine room was oddly warm, and tools were scattered about. But this time the toolbox was magically filled up with all the rusted tools we had found the previous day, the ones we had locked up in the museum! That day I found the two locks broken open in the field around the sub like they had been thrown. I decided not to sleep on the ship anymore.

I later found out the ashes of a cook and a mechanic are buried on the boat. The mechanic took no shit, and the cook liked to prank people when he was still alive. There's also a man that apparently sings in the aft torpedo room. But I never saw him. Rumor has it that females during tours feel hands groping them. Over a dozen females have claimed this after their tours. It seems to always happen between the galley and engine room.

Fort McCoy

I was at Fort McCoy, Wisconsin for ROM before Navy Boot Camp in March 2021. Towards the last few days of our two-week quarantine, I was on watch at like 0000-0200. It was hot in our building, so most guys slept with the windows open. My petty officer came downstairs and told me it would rain later that night, so that when it started, I should close the windows.

So I'm standing there on watch, looking out a window, and I see a blue light I hadn't seen before off in the distance. I don't think anything of it until it vanishes, then appears just a little closer, and then again and again.

This continues all night until it's right across the street from my building. At this point, I'm seriously considering if I should write "watch stander abducted by aliens" in the deck log. About this time, it starts raining, so I have to unglue myself from my post and shut the windows. Well, I'm going down the row, closing the windows, and I get to the one in the very back right corner. I reach behind the blinds to close the window.

No sooner than I reached my hand back did something knock several times against the outside wall. I took off running back to the other side of the building and woke up my relief 10 minutes early. I don't know what did it, but the other guys in my building said that they had seen shadows and heard footsteps at night. All I can say is that Fort McCoy is haunted.

NAF Atsugi

I was at NAF Atsugi, Japan, from 2004-2006. The history of Atsugi is a fabled one. Set up in 1938 by Japan, Atsugi was home to the 302d Naval Air Group or Kokutai, which was tasked with the air defense of Tokyo. It was also said to be the last air group to see combat against American forces on the morning of August 15, 1945, the day of the surrender was announced.

After Japan's Surrender announcement by Hirohito, it is believed the commander of the 302d had all available planes take off into the air to drop leaflets on Tokyo and Yokohama, instructing locals to resist the allied forces. The pilots, however, never returned to base, with their final destinations unknown (presumably crashed).

After the surrender, Gen. Douglas MacArthur landed at Atsugi to accept the formal surrender of the Empire of Japan on the morning of 30 August 1945. The signing of the treaty was held in Tokyo Bay on 2 September 1945. There are several tunnels and cave systems throughout the base the Japanese built throughout the war. I don't know to where or how far these tunnels went.

It was in one of these tunnels that I had my "odd" experience. I was a young Master-at-Arms and one night, while on duty, all the mobile patrols decided to explore (uh I mean patrol) the tunnels and caves around the base. One of the guys brought along his video camera. It was about 0300 and we explored (I mean patrolled) for about an hour or so. We saw some odd things down there but no apparitions or anything that screamed paranormal.

When we came out, we reviewed the tape from the video camera, and what we saw shocked us. As we were walking into the cave, we saw on the video a noose hanging from the entrance with a body attached. However, there was no face. This was only captured on the camera, and we did not see it with our naked eyes. The best way to describe it was a blur covering the face, and we were unable to make out facial features.

The body was dressed in all white. We think we bumped it because as we are walking past: we see it hanging still, but the guy with the camera turns to those behind him to tell them something, and when he turns, the body is swaying heavily left to right in the frame. After seeing this video, we all got into our patrol cars and went faster than we could say, "boo." I do not know whatever happened to that tape as I lost touch with the guy who filmed it because he was discharged shortly afterward, and this was just before social media became popular.

I wish I had asked for a copy, but I was so shocked by that tape. I asked some other buddies about that night that I still keep in contact with, but nobody seems to know where the cameraman went after leaving the service. Could it have been the spirit of a Japanese aviator who committed suicide in the war's final days or a captured Allied POW? Could it be a U.S. Service member who committed suicide after the battle? We will never know. We never went into the caves ever again.

Annapolis

I got a story from when I was a midshipman at the Naval Academy up in Annapolis. There are tons of people I went to school with and worked with who had weird experiences in Bancroft Hall (the dorm where all of the students live). Anyway, it's just before the beginning of the fall semester of my senior year. I have a bs job on my battalion's staff (I just make watch bills), and our commander wants to meet with the new staff members in preparation for the beginning of the school year.

The summer staff occupied the conference room we would generally use. So we used an empty office across our battalion's conference room—nothing special about the office, just a square room with a couple of chairs and a desk. One door goes into the building's main hallway and a window on the opposite wall.

I get there a few minutes early and start catching up with my friends who are also on the staff (everyone was returning from leave/training, so none of us had seen each other in a few months). While I'm standing there talking with my back to the door, but a solid 8 ft into the room, I feel someone tap me on my right hip and whisper "Hey" into my left ear. Assuming it's either some other staff member or a friend who happened to walk by and see me in the room, I turn and say, "Hey, what's up."

But there's nobody either in the room behind me or visible through the door into the hallway. I know I'm too far into the room for someone to have been able to get passed me before I turned around, and everyone else in the room was along the wall with the window (too far away to have done anything without me noticing). At this point, a shiver goes down my spine, and I turn back to the other people and ask if someone had been behind me. They all look at me confused and say, "No." I kept it together for the meeting, but I never went back to that office again.

Sands of Iwo Jima

My story revolves around sands of Iwo Jima, not the John Wayne movie, but literal sand from Iwo Jima. Iwo Jima is one of the most famous battles of WWII, which produced the iconic photo of six Marines taken by Joe Rosenthal atop Mount Suribachi. Around 2005, we were allowed to go to Iwo on TDY for about 10-14 days.

As Master at Arms and part of NAF Atsugi's security forces, we would follow CVW-5 and explain why they did workups or used the island for night landing practices. It was a great opportunity and a real eye-opener history lesson. There is no civilian population, and the only Americans on the island come in when the CVW is on the Island. The Japanese have a permanent party there for airfield operations and such.

Much of the island is stuck in a time capsule and looks just as it did during the gruesome battle of 1945. Medical caves with bandages, morphine, bloody gauze, bullet holes in the rocks, rusted-out cannons, and gun mounts. You can see where the Japanese looked down on the invasion beach as the Marines came ashore. The Japanese Government has strictly prohibited ANY artifacts from being taken from the Island. If it did not go with you to Iwo, it stays on Iwo. This includes sand, rocks, and water, or other artifacts. One of the people we went with decided to collect some sand in a jar from invasion beach.

After the TDY and back on the mainland, she put the sand she collected on the window sill in her barracks room. After returning from work, she found it had fallen off the window sill onto her bed. She didn't think anything of it, chalked it up to someone having the bass too loud upstairs or an earthquake or something while she was at work, and inadvertently got knocked over with the vibration. So she set it on her stationary desk. She went to bed, got up to get ready for her next shift, and while she was asleep, the jar had fallen again off the desk and landed on the chair.

Again, she picked it up, placed it on the desk in the middle away from the edges, didn't think anything of it, and went to work. When she returned from work again, the was jar knocked off the desk, this time though it was clear across her room and the top of the jar had been opened, and sand was spilled everywhere. It was at this moment she knew she messed up. She quickly got her vacuum and cleaned up as soon as possible and threw the vacuum out along with the jar. I'm surprised she didn't start ripping out the carpet as well.

UNITED STATES MARINE CORPS

OKINAWA AND JAPAN

Cries From The Jungle

Seeing your stories has motivated me to tell my own story. I used to work day and night in the Muns area of Kadena (big jungle area next to the base). Easu to get lost in, and it is a thick jungle that barely lets the light through on the brightest of days.

Anyways one night, it's a little after 0100, and we are parking our 7ton truck in our gated area. Winds are blowing stronger than usual, and I'm holding the gate while my LCpl is parking the truck, and my SSgt is ground guiding. Despite all the noise from the wind and truck, I start to hear a baby's cry.

Not like an animal or something but a legitimate cry from a baby in the jungle about 50m from us. I have no idea why I thought it was a good idea, but I started walking towards the jungle, thinking I would rescue this baby. My SSgt yelled at me to come back, and at the exact moment, the cry stopped. I got this incredibly eerie feeling from the jungle.

I told him what I heard, and he said he's heard to the same thing before but figured nothing good comes out of the jungle at night. The next day I'm talking with some of the other guys, and one of them tells me that the previous year he and another Marine were driving by the same area and almost crashed their truck after the driver swerved because of a baby in the middle of the road.

Others had seen or heard things in that jungle. Dudes have heard Japanese voices in the wilderness, babies crying out in the darkness, and have seen people walking around.

It makes sense since Okinawa had so much intense fighting and so many lives lost there. The whole island is spooky.

The Hidden Camp Hansen

My best bud and I were pulling post at midnight on Camp Hansen's single lane MOUT. We were standing in an empty COC-like room with all our SESM uppers, 240s, rounds, radios, etc. I'm sitting in there when my best bud comes back from roving, and I go out to rove. I thought I saw one of my Marines, who towers over me at 6 foot 6, stand up real slow from behind the medical vehicle and start waving at me. I was walking up to him to tell him to get some rest, and then the next second, he just wasn't there.

I walked into the bivouac and found my Marine sound asleep on his cot. After I left there, I went to walk down the road (Hansen MOUT is one lane), and I saw people walking up and down the street, riding bicycles, disappearing through walls, the whole nine yards. The best way to describe them is that they looked like they were wearing invisibility cloaks from Harry Potter.

I thought I was tripping, so I flipped down my NVGs (yep still there), and just turned around to go back and tell my best bud. He goes out too and saw the same people going through walls and shit. We chalked it up to sleep deprivation because we drove to the Camp Schwab ASP at 0300 the previous morning, but we probably got about 10 hours of sleep and downtime after that.

Anyways, the weird, quiet Marine in our platoon reported seeing eight-foot figures in the fake church on the left side of the MOUT lane. We experienced unexplainable radio chatter, someone thought they heard someone using an old phonetic alphabet over the net. We saw skinny shadows no bigger than a twig passing in front of our gate guard vehicle in the pouring rain at night. We heard sounds in the building, gate guards saw people walk past the gates into MOUT, shadows were moving through the hygiene area during sunrise, there was some sketchy shit going on. I think that whole island is a haunted graveyard.

Haunted Barracks at Camp Schwab

So I was on a UDP and Camp Schwab for this story. The whole company goes to the Philippines; three dudes from headquarters and two guys from Easy Co are left in the entire barracks. That's when it starts getting weird. Every day I did laundry (middle of summer Oki sweat issues), the doors for every dryer were open.

I was on the top floor, and the headquarters guys were the rooms by me. I'd go back to get my laundry out, and they are all open. I shut all the doors every time, and then they would be open when I came back. I hear if the other guys on the floor would open or close their doors. So one night I was in there, just shut the doors, and out the corner of my eye was a solid white figure, but once I looked, it was gone.

Whatever. So I go back to get my laundry, and as I'm kneeling, I feel someone run their hand across my head. I have a shaved head, and there is a distinct difference between a hand and wind on my head. Later I'm lying-in bed that night, and suddenly the guy in the room across from me is banging on my door and yelling for me to open the door.

I let him in and asked what the fuck was going on. He said he had a dream, and this lady in all white was grabbing him, yelling to come with her, and when he shoved her away, the metal vent cover crashed down on his ceiling.

For anyone who never lived in Oki barracks, you have to push up and twist for them to come down. I went over with him and checked, and the vent was there on the floor, and his shoes were gone. Turning a camera light on under his bed, they were all pushed into the corner of the room under his bed. He kept his shoes aligned like he was a recruit still, so this wasn't normal.

I started asking him if he had been experiencing weird things, and he said yes. The next day we asked the few others in the barracks and they also said yes. When everyone came back, it went away. I take it the ghost didn't have the energy to haunt some 300 Marines, but the few of us were prime targets.

Ghostly Girl Of Camp Schwab

So I never witnessed the girl ghost, but my Staff Sergeant saw her on the first UDP he was on. When I replaced my buddies during my UDP, they told me they saw her as well. From what I was told back in the '70s or 80' a 7 ton killed a little girl in that area, and she's haunted that area ever since.

In our first UDP in '14, my SSgt was on Battalion Staff Duty, and he and the duty driver were heading down to the ramp late at night to double-check everything was locked. From what he said, they pull up to the gate at the ramp, and he gets out and starts to get the gate unlocked. He looks up, and about 30 feet away, next to the last line of AAVs, there's this Japanese girl ghost looking at him and the duty driver. She then walks past the AVVs, through the fence, and disappears into the jungle. My SSgt said, fuck that, and they hauled back to the battalion building

In 2016 I arrived a month early to do change over with the other company. I'm hanging out with my buddy, and he tells me that the prior week they were in the bay working on a track. It's late at night and pouring rain, there's about a half dozen of them working on getting this track fixed.

He said they all just turned and looked out to the line of LAVs and AAVs, and there's the girl ghost looking at them. Once they see her, she turns and walks through the line of vehicles and the fence back into the jungle. They all bounced and didn't want to hang around after that. I know some more of the guys I had been with had witnessed this ghost, but those are the two that I recall in detail. We were always spooked if we were out there late at night.

Some of the instructors would talk about getting old radio transmissions from WW2 when they were in Okinawa. They told us if we get to Okinawa and are doing night ops, we might run into that while we were there.

Camp Schwab Barracks

I couldn't tell you exactly when it happened, just that it was on Camp Schwab at the 4th Marines barracks, probably in April, around 0200-0300. Nothing before this would have ever left me to believe my barracks were haunted. Schwab had a handful of cats and dogs running loose and one morning on my way in, a dog caught me off guard barking and jump-scared the hell out of me coming over a hill - that was the extent of scary things I figured would happen.

I don't particularly remember what woke me up. I remember coming to and being 100% awake, no eye rubbing or yawning, just bam awake - and unable to move anything other than my head. I turned right and could feel this presence watching me. My bed was positioned on the back wall, so it was the first thing you'd see if you entered the room. I could see the faint outlines -of a shadow, about the size of a person, this thing felt evil.

It felt like it was after me, and God only knew what it would do to me if it got to me. I started to pray. I'm not religious, but I've read into a few different religions out of curiosity. I prayed to every deity that came to mind for help. I finally was able to build up the courage to sit up in bed, get dressed, and go past it out of the room. My praying seemed to have held it in place while I quickly walked past it. I made it out past the duty, and they asked me why I was awake.

I proceeded to tell him, thinking he will never believe me, but he does. Oddly enough, one of my buddies came up and recounted he felt tired earlier in the night, but something within himself told me he needed to stay awake a while longer. We all ended up going back to my room, and this entity was gone by the time we returned.

I had later heard rumors of people on base throughout its long history practicing black magic, but who knows if that's true or not. I never heard from anyone else during my time on the rock if they experienced anything similar. I recently read a post on this page about someone else at LAR having something similar happen to them. It gives me the creeps thinking about it all, but at least I know I'm not 100% crazy.

"I didn't know you spoke Spanish"

I was with 3rd LAR at Camp Schwab, Okinawa. Before I say the story, sometimes I have sleep paralysis. It's not always a constant thing in my life, but it comes and goes. It's maybe 6 or 7 am on a Saturday and I'm asleep in my barracks room. My bed is alongside a wall, and you can see the wall lockers from it as well as the little entrance into the room where the sink would be. It has some dim yellowish-green light, and it's not very bright.

Anyways I wake up at like 0600 or 0700, and of course, I am caught in an episode of sleep paralysis. I felt something staring at me, so I look towards the entrance of the room. I see some weird black smoke or mist, almost transparent. Right away, my entire body starts to shake and tremble, and the first thing that comes to my mind is that a demon is trying to possess me.

I'm a guy of Christian faith, so I start praying, and it suddenly stops. I open my eyes, and it's still there, but this time it's closer. I lay there for several minutes with my eyes shut. I can smell the scent of something rotting, so I keep praying, and finally it feels like it stops for good. My roommate looks over at me and says: "Bro, you were sleep talking. I didn't know you spoke Spanish."

I don't speak Spanish. I now believe he heard me speaking Latin, but I don't know Latin, nor have I ever heard it spoken. I read somewhere that the scent of something rotting can point towards a demonic apparition. So yeah, scary stuff.

GITMO

Whistling On Guantanamo Bay

I was deployed to Guantanamo Bay, Cuba, in the late 2000s. We were told ghost stories about some of the towers along the base perimeter we Marines would man. I would usually staff the building across the bay that overlooked the ocean and see the airfield (I can't remember the name, opposite side of the main base).

People off duty would occasionally run to the building for PT. I'd always hear footsteps walking up the tower, I'd look to see who was stopping by to visit, and usually there was someone stopping buy. But occasionally, there would be footsteps coming up the tower and I would look to the stairs… but when the footsteps stopped there would be no one.

One day I heard whistling at the bottom of the tower, like someone was whistling a toon. I couldn't make it out very well, but then I heard footsteps coming up the tower. The whistling got louder as the footsteps got closer to the top. I looked all around and didn't see anyone. The footsteps and whistling suddenly stopped about 3/4 of the way up. Never saw anyone.

I never heard the whistling again but I still heard footsteps walking up the tower occasionally. Sometimes to then closed door, and I'd wait for the door to open by itself. But it never did though.

Ghostly Encounters At GITMO

I was a fence line guard in GITMO in 2000. We heard a bunch of stories of ghosts. Mysterious sightings: the headless gunnery sergeant, the woman in the river that lost her daughter escaping Cuba, etc., certain towers were more haunted than others. I would spend a lot of time in those towers, and most of the time, it was pretty peaceful. One day we had a gnarly tropical storm come through, and I received the previous Marine from the last rotation who was thoroughly soaked and tired.

I set up my gear, did a radio check, and settled in for a long uncomfortable night staring at the other side. That night I had a red light in the building on (I usually would have it off and would sit in the dark while scanning with NVG's). I had been there for several hours, and the storm had died down. A low fog had crept in, and there were random lightning strikes in the hills around the base. As I was sitting there in the darkness I began to see ghostly figures low crawling and walking below my tower. I was confused but too tired to care, I just stared not knowing what to think.

Out of nowhere, I heard a man's voice telling me to remove my batteries from my light and shut my main radio off. The voice told me that he needed the batteries outside. I was fatigued and not thinking straight: I pulled my batteries, shut off my radio, and then walked out of the tower with batteries in hand. Keep in mind the tower was prob like forty feet high with a short railing around the perimeter. I walked out, and the sudden darkness snapped me out of it. I was standing there looking down the steep stairs that led down completely confused.

I heard the voice again, bright and clear, like the Sgt of the guard had just ordered me to do something. I came to my senses, walked back inside, did another radio check, and spent the rest of the night wondering what I had just experienced.

What makes this even weirder was that the following day, I told my buddy what had happened. His eyes opened up wide, and he asked me if I was joking. When I told him I wasn't joking, he proceeded to tell me the same thing happened to him the very same night in another tower.

I heard a lot of stories like mine when I was there. You could look in old logbooks and read where guys had to get pulled off post because they were flipping out over voices and sightings. There's a lot of history and tragedy around that base. I think about it every so often, and I'm not particularly superstitious. What tripped me out was that my buddy experienced the same thing. Who knows, the world is a mysterious place.

Little Girl At Gitmo

In 2013 I was in Guantanamo Bay with my infantry platoon guarding the base's fence line. The platoon we were relieving told us stories of a ghost on one of the posts, but we all thought they were trying to scare us.

A few weeks after we started standing post by ourselves, the guys on 0000-0800 posts began complaining about being scared of their positions. No one thought anything of it.

My good friend was standing on a post that was notoriously "haunted," one that everyone complained about it. One night I was the SOG, just driving around in my pickup when he radioed me to come to his tower. I head over and climb the stairs, and I find him sitting in the corner of the room with his rifle pointed at the door.

I ask him, "What's wrong?" He (obviously freaked out) replies, "Someone is out there, man. Someone that is not human. It's walking THROUGH things." So I start thinking, "Wow, these night shifts are starting to fuck with people." I spend some time with him, and then we get a phone call. I walk over to the phone box, open it, and answer, "Lance Corporal Blah blah." No answer.

The line goes dead, and so I call all the other posts that are active and see if it was them. No one said they called. I'm pretty sure my call woke all of them up! So, the only other option is the call came from one of the unmanned towers, and the only other tower with a phone is right down the road. I get in my pickup and head that way, suspecting it's a Cuban who just crossed the fence and wants to be picked up and detained.

I arrive at the post, and it's noticeably colder by a lot. This is Cuba.

168

The temperature at night is pretty warm since it's on the equator, and I could see my breath. I walk up to the post and have to shove the door open. There are dead leaves and dirt all over the floor. No one had been inside of it for months…except the phone box was open…and the phone was dangling.

Then I get another call over the radio from my buddy. He said the thing was back. I get back in my pickup and race to the post. I run up the stairs, and open the door. When I get through the threshold of the door, it slams shut behind me. Immediately I start to freak out. We spend some time in the tower together trying to figure out what's going on, and eventually, I decide to leave

As I'm walking down the stairs, I round the corner in the square pattern the stairs were made on, and at the very bottom of the tower is what appeared to be a child. But the child is all white and translucent. By the time it takes me to draw my pistol, the child is gone. I looked up, and my buddy was poking his head out of the tower and said, "I saw all of that. You aren't crazy!"

AT WAR AND DEPLOYED

Africa

I deployed to Africa. My base had been attacked a few weeks prior, so we were working every day, and I was exhausted. For more context, I worked nights the whole time. That place was naturally creepy at night with hyenas, bugs and snakes. One night, I was in my tower sitting down, and I felt a human hand grab my shoulder and shake me. I freak out and turn around (we were in blackout, mind you). I see nothing. I look through my NVGs and thermals and can't find anything.

It was an aggressive shake. It was also hot and humid at night, but when this happened, I felt the temperature noticeably get colder. I'm not superstitious, but that did feel like something not ordinary. Additionally, my buddy had a nearly identical experience in the same tower which is also about 20ft or so off the ground. The only way up is a ladder. If anyone did climb up there, you would have heard them on the aluminum ladder.

Some of my buddies also had some weird experiences out there. One guy thought he saw someone climbing the fence, but it could only be seen through thermals, which was pretty odd because only one guy saw it without thermals. It was a shadow figure of sorts. The real creepy story however, was a friend who said he saw a shadow figure walk out from the wood line and stare at him. This shadowy figure was just staring him down. He felt it was a security risk and he and a few others drew weapons. But before anyone could say anything, this figure disappears in thin air.

Djibouti

An airfield in Kenya was hit by Al Shabaab early in January. That's its own fucked up story that isn't very spooky. My buddy and I get down there with the QRF.

They didn't have space for us, so we slept in and around the hanger on the airfield. One night I'm watching the airport, and I see a shadowy figure slowly pop out of some bushes. I didn't know if it was a man or an animal. It just looked like a black mass.

I swear I saw the thing take off and sprint towards us. Someone yells, "Hey, Stop!" I blink my eyes, and the thing has vanished. There was a lot of "did you see that... what the fuck was that?".

When we got back to Djibouti, I was bullshitting with one of the 101st guys, and he was telling me that during the attack, one of the African security force guys dropped his weapon and ran into the jungle. Supposedly when he was found eight hours later, he was hugging a tree and mumbling about the shadow man who chased him.

FOB Delhi

FOB Delhi Garmsir District circa 2012, our Chaplain swore there was this ancient and evil apparition that would appear along the hesco barrier wall that ran along the Helmand River.

The apparition allegedly was a male in traditional Muslim garb but with soulless black pits for eyes and an abnormally large, gaping mouth with fucked up teeth. The rumor was that there was a sight of an old burial ground where this apparition was seen.

No one believed the Chaplain, but interestingly enough we had a camera on that wall of the FOB that we could control with a remote from the COC. Every so often, usually at night, the camera would glitch and move on its own to focus on the exact spot in question along the river. Of course, someone would have to go over to it and manually reset the camera, which was always creepy as fuck, but to my knowledge, no one ever saw anything.

Lights Over Makhmur

I was deployed in 2016 to Makhmur, Iraq, Firebase Bell (shoutout to the Guardsmen and Marines who fought there). We were always on 24-hour ops hitting Mosul and as a result, sleep-deprived. But keep in mind once you see the same weird thing a bunch of times and the whole platoon sees the exact same thing, it's probably not a hallucination.

We saw these green lights. Like little balls of green fire in groups. They looked like flare dumps from a gunship or helo. The skies were pitch black from the burning oil fields. But there were these green balls of light. As I said, it looked like green flares with no aircraft soaring through the sky. It didn't seem mechanical. Floating more than flying, but faster than any flare I had seen.

I saw it on guard at 0300 against the oily sky, with no NVGs. I looked at my partner and was like, "you saw that?" He said, "yep." We didn't say anything else about it.

We never really talked about it or questioned it, lots more to worry about in Northern Iraq. But every few nights, we would see them, flying or falling in clumps and disappearing over the mountain or horizon. Other guys from the platoon would see them and mention them in the morning.

Camp Leatherneck UFOs

My unit had gotten there from KAF like a month before, and while we were building the camp, they needed volunteers for base security/QRF. I was first posted guarding the COC within Leatherneck, where General Nicholson was at, and all the high-ranking officers and alphabets were working out of. I was just there checking IDs and got to talk to some of them.

One night, we were just chilling, and minding our own business. It was a regular night, and it's not busy at all when I started pacing around and suddenly looked up in the distance. I saw like three to four orange/reddish orbs floating. I just stared at them a little bit and was like, "what the fuck is that?"

172

At first, I thought they were maybe flares or maybe aircraft lined up, but why would they be round and orange. They seemed to be far off in the distance, but you could see them clearly from where we were. So I called my post buddy up and asked, "Hey, you see this?" We just stared at it like idiots for maybe like 10 min, and then all of a sudden, another row of three to four orbs popped out below them. Maybe another 10 min went by, and four more would appear under them. Suddenly, these orbs of light began to float around each other.

As we're checking IDs, we're trying to figure this out. We started pointing them out and asking around (majors, captain, one SSgt) and everyone was just as baffled. It couldn't have been flares because flares don't dance around each other and stay up there for what lasts literally hours.

I thought it was just a cool, little, dumb UFO story for me until a couple of years later, the Marine times posted something with a picture of EXACTLY what I saw. So it confirmed that my buddy and I weren't crazy, and more people saw it.

The only difference was that the article was about someone seeing it in 2011, and I was in Afghan in 2009. I think I had tried taking a picture of it with either my terrible digital camera or my phone at the time, which I think was just a shitty blackberry. But have no idea where either of them are.

They were almost dancing around each other. Like four more would pop out of nowhere after 30 min, then four more, they would float and stay up there while moving around each other. There were maybe 10-15 orbs just hanging out. Almost felt like they were watching us.

Fallujah

US Marine. You need Fallujah stories. That place was evil. That was my first deployment; I relieved the guys from 3/5, who were a part of Operation Phantom Fury. They probably made some ghosts. That whole city felt like walking into a haunted house.

On the outside of Fallujah, was a place called Camp Bahria. It's at the center of two deep artificial lakes ringed by roads and cottages. We didn't know this at first but this originally was lodging for Saddam's son's prostitutes.

This became the spot for our leadership and a place to be outside Fallujah for using the PX and taking showers. In order to guard this large base in the middle of the desert, every company had to give up guys. Besides the headquarters Marines, the guards came from our unit.

I head back to Camp Bahria. I haven't showered or eaten real food in a month, so I'm excited about that. As soon as I get there, I see guys I haven't seen in a while, and they tell me some scary stories about the place. Like pulling skeletons out of the lake, but the scariest is this...

The guys on guard duty man six-hour posts. One of these posts is a two-story shack with stairs that wrap around it. So 0300 a guy up and hears a noise. He looks down the stairs and sees an Iraqi girl. She begins walking up the stairs and he screams.

As she is walking up, she begins to get older and older with each step as she gets closer. By the time she's face to face with him, she's an old lady. Then suddenly, in an instant, she's right in his face. He was found terrified and cowering in the corner, his finger was still on his SAW and a burst of rounds covered the opposite wall.

That place is evil.

No Myth Here

I'm a Sgt in the USMC and a 0311 basic infantryman. In February 2011, we were doing a NATO training exercise in Norway. One night in the Norwegian mountains, we were in the process of bedding down for the night.

Getting the last smoke in before bed, I and several US and Norwegian Marines heard a loud howl, more of a yowl, coming from up the mountain.

174

I've heard wolves, coyotes, and dogs before. Heard cougars too. That was nothing I had heard before. When I turned to look at the Norwegian Marines, they all looked terrified.

Someone jokingly said it's a Yeti. The Norwegians responded with, "It is. Yeti is very real, and we need to be careful. Not myth very real."

Then they left and went to bed. It was a crazy weird night. At first, we blew it off as them messing with us. But we reconsidered once we saw how dead serious they were and how they looked cautiously up the mountain.

Syria

In 2018 I was on a joint firebase in Syria with about a platoon of Marines (unit omitted for privacy). We took the base, an old hotel-spa type thing, from ISIS back in about 2016.

They used several buildings in the larger compound as a makeshift jail. We heard stories about torture and other horrible acts in these jails; we saw things carved into the walls. One of the cells had the "evil eye" carved into the wall by one of the former prisoner's fingernails. This was DEEP in the wall of a concrete building for context. I recognized the symbol, though it was creepy but thought nothing of it and moved on.

We ended up placing a post with several machine guns on top of the jail cell with the evil eye symbol, and that's when things started to get weird. At night a few guys mentioned hearing voices of a child and women crying behind them and down in the jail cell. I didn't know if they were messing around or not, but I decided to go up there on my own the next night.

The next night I went up there and joked around/shot the shit with the guys up there for a while. Then out of nowhere, we heard something move the gate below, which blocked the entrance to the post. I grabbed my M4 and went down to investigate (thought maybe a cat or one of the Kurds looking for cigarettes or something). I found the gate, a big heavy metal gate, now open wide.

When I went to close it, I felt an immediate sense of dread and darkness slide up behind me. I can't describe how horrible I felt and how cold I got at that moment. I was scared to turn around and even if I found nothing, I had a terrible feeling that the evil eye on the wall there was projecting pure hate in my direction.

I went back up to the post faster than I'd like to admit and thought up an excuse to get the hell out of there. I heard crying off behind the building where I lived and slept at night, so I decided to stay in the post with the safety of the other Marines. I stayed there until the sun was up and then stayed up the entire next day. I tried my best to spend as little time in that post after that. Most of the other guys admitted to hearing and feeling similar things throughout that deployment.

STATESIDE

The Little Girl At Camp Lejeune

When I was stationed at Lejeune around 2016, I had FAPed over to PMO. We just switched to overnight hours, which begin at 1700 and usually lasted until about 0600 or so depending on the situation. This event occurred around 0200 or 0300.

If you have ever been stationed at Lejeune, you're most likely familiar with the Sneads Ferry back gate entrance located south of the base. There's nothing but a waterway and forest for miles once you enter. Right before the entry point, there's a small bus stop located on the right as soon as you cross over the bridge.

So around 0200-0300 we get a call to dispatch from the sentry that he sees a small child running around the bus stop singing and laughing (keep in mind it's pitch black and the closest house is over the long bridge). Dispatch repeats his call to clarify the situation, and the sentry is told to make contact with the little girl. The sentry acknowledged dispatch, and there was radio silence for a few minutes.

About five to ten minutes pass, and the sentry radios back to dispatch. He tried to make contact with the little girl, but as he got closer, she kept singing more and more, and she started to retreat into the shadows until she disappeared. Neither the sentry or his partner saw the little girl the rest of the night, but they made sure not to leave the guard shack until sunrise. We never really looked into it, but with the accidents around the area, it's possible she could have been a fatality from a car crash.

We had another call from the same guard shack reporting they kept seeing a "shadow" person in the camera, and every time the sentry would go out to check, it would disappear.

There are some other stories about that bridge. For example, a woman committed suicide years ago and allegedly at night, you can hear screams coming from the bridge. That whole area at night is creepy especially when you have to patrol solo.

Camp Pendleton Barracks Terror

My old barracks room in the Marines was a living nightmare. I got so many stories, but I'll type up the first occurrence.

I was stationed on Camp Pendleton at the time and grew up close to there, so I'd often go to my parents' house on the weekends and even some weeknights. If I went home, I'd wake up around 0430-0500 in the morning and drive back on base for PT. If I got there early with time to spare, I'd take a nap in my barracks room. This was one of those mornings. I shared the barracks room with a roommate, but he was home on leave at the time.

I was napping in my room when I felt someone shake me awake. I sat up in bed, a little confused. My very first thought was that my mom was shaking me awake at home because I overslept or something.

But I was in my barracks room, so I brushed it off and laid back down. I was lying on my side with my back to the wall. Shortly after I closed my eyes, I felt something sit on the edge of the bed in front of my feet. I thought my brain must be playing tricks on me, but then I felt this thing get up, walk around the bed and sit down behind my feet now.

So, it's now sitting between my feet and the wall. I'm creeped out. I'm still lying there wide awake but my eyes are closed and trying to not react. Then I feel this thing start CRAWLING up the bed. I feel the bed indenting as their hands and knees move up the bed.

I'm telling myself to let it get to my head and see what happens. But it gets to my belly button, and I freak out. I throw my hand over there and flip the lights on. There's nothing there, of course, so I take off and nap in my car. I kept trying to rationalize what it was in my head, thinking it's like a cat or a rat. But not matter how much I try; I can't explain what it was.

Fort Des Moines

I don't have a dramatic story about witnessing a paranormal entity in Afghanistan or a Skinwalker out in the woods at night. But the experience I'm about to share is corroborated by another Marine who experienced the same thing on a separate occasion.

It was June 2019, Fort Des Moines, Des Moines, IA. To call the former USMC building within the Army Reserve base at Fort Des Moines "ancient" would not be an understatement. The tiny outpost itself dates back to 1843 and played a relatively insignificant role in training officers and even some of the first females to have a meaningful role in the military during the Second World War.

The actual USMC building within Fort Des Moines was creaky, underdeveloped, and made out of an old horse stable. Nothing you'd really see in the FMF, but the place obviously had some history.

I drove into the fort that afternoon to square my gear away before an upcoming field op. I barely gained access to the building because one lonely I&I Marine allowed me to enter and claimed he was soon leaving. I said okay, and carried on up to my platoon room.

The long hallway I had to shuffle down was dark. Real fucking dark. Only the glowing red exit signs in the hallways illuminated my path. I quickly walked down that hallway and into the lighted safety of my weapons platoon room. I packed my gear like any other Marine and was about to depart, but I heard the familiar of footsteps coming up the back stairwell.

Rapid footsteps that sounded as if someone was jogging up and down the stairs. I stared in the direction of the steps for what seemed like minutes. The chills and a feeling of "what the fuck?" began to set in. But I brushed it off, stowed my gear away, and made for my car quickly down that dark hallway. But, one thing was missing when I finally reached the safety of day light: any signs of cars or other marines in the parking lot. The place was abandoned and the I&I Marine had no reason to even go near the back stairwell for any reason.

Before this happened, a similar story was told to me by another marine who actually spent the night here. Initially ignored it as an NCO trying to entertain himself with the gullible characteristics of his subordinates. But after my experience, I believed him. Thank God I left that place.

Camp Pendleton Hogan Barracks

I had come down to relieve my DNCO at 0100 and for about an hour, I'm just chilling in the 62 areas Hogan Barracks duty hut. The way the duty desk faces is towards a laundry room with windows. The laundry room has motion detector lights as well.

It's all dark in there and I'm on my phone when I see someone move from right to left inside, away from the room entrance, but the lights don't turn on. I get a little curious and walk over to check it out. I open the door, and the lights instantly turn on. No one is there. I walk through and even check the little janitor's closet, and not a sign of a person.

I'm a little creeped out and I'm pacing around the duty desk. So I started looking into all the tiny rooms that connect to the main common area, like a theater and a kitchen. Then I go into an unused computer room full of boxes of linen, it's completely dark in there. I find the light switch and look around, then turn it off and step back outside the room.

The second my foot goes outside the threshold of the door, the door of the duty bunk room behind the duty desk slams shut. This door has been cracked open all day and just now slams with no explanation.

I'm completely on edge and decide to get the fuck out, and I go to the CP where one of the Sgts I'm friendly with is on duty. I tell him what happened, and he says, "no way." He was sitting at his desk and swore he saw someone walk from room to room but ignored it until I came in.

About an hour later, I searched around, but there was nothing in the bunk room except pillows and couches. I hope I never get duty in there again.

The Glitch

US Marine. So, unlike most stories that I've read on your platform, this isn't an alien or cryptid story. This story is more of a "glitch in the matrix" type story or event that happened to me.

This event took place in 29 Palms, California. It's a Marine base in the Mojave Desert about three hours away from Las Vegas. It tends to get hot as fuck during the day and cold as fuck during the night. During this time, me and my buddy were undergoing our training to become Comms Marines. We picked up in the same class, so we spent a lot of time together. One of those times was at night in question.

We had gotten out of class for the day we walked back from evening chow. Our rooms were in the second barracks between the first and the third, also known as the BMAT barracks. When we had reached the bottom stairs, my buddy looked at me, and initiated a race up to the second floor where our rooms were at. He had a head start, but he wasn't too far from me. I looked down at the stairs because I was skipping stairs. I reached the top of the stairs, and I looked up, expecting to see my buddy standing next to me.

But he wasn't there, I searched around the corner expecting him to jump out at me, and he wasn't there either. I went across the hall and up to the third floor, calling his name without answering. I even went back down the stairs. I know I was calling out loud because one of the rooms had the curtains open, and the people inside were making rude gestures motioning me to be quiet. I gave up and thought maybe my buddy had made it into his room somehow.

On my way back, my name was called right behind me. I turned around, and it was my buddy. We are both confused. After we talked, I found out that from his perspective, he had been standing at the top of the 2nd-floor stairs the entire time waiting for me.

This is where it gets weird. The staircase is not that wide, so even if

I hadn't seen him, my battle buddy is a big guy, so I would've bumped into him if I ran up the stairs head-on.

But neither of us saw each other. I was calling out his name, and I knew it was loud enough to hear it because of the people in the room, but he said he heard nothing. He also said that he had called me, but I had heard nothing. We were freaked out about it, and we told the rest of our classmates, but they didn't believe us or just brushed us off.

However, this part of the story makes me believe there was something more to it. A couple of days later, our story had reached the ears of our instructor. He asked me about it, and I told him what had happened. Expecting him to make light of it and brush it off as a joke like everyone else, I wasn't serious in retelling the story. That was, until I saw his expression. He became serious, looked me dead in the eye, and said, "Do not talk about this anymore."

I don't know what he was trying to hide or if this was something government-related. I know this story doesn't seem like much, but it is a reoccurring topic my battle buddy and I still talk about. We still speculate about what happened that day, like maybe one of us slipped into a wormhole to another dimension or something. But it happened, and I know there's something more to it.

Dugway Proving Grounds

During my time in the Marines, I served as a CBRN (chemical, biological, radiological, and nuclear) defense specialist, basically the dude that teaches other Marines how to use a gas mask and additional PPE. I once got orders to Dugway Proving Grounds for a multilateral equipment test for some new HazMat kit the military was interested in.

For those who aren't familiar with Dugway, it's the neighbor training grounds to Area 51, also known as Area 52. It's a highly classified area with areas authorized to use deadly force, this place is home to drone research and defense, chemical/bioresearch, and probably a few other things now.

During my time there for all exercises, I was team leader for the first reconnaissance. My job was to take the team downrange and report back the initial conditions, samples, etc. Nothing crazy. The night before one of the tests, the guys decided to the "go-to" bar for drinks. This bar rocked a four-foot-tall alien statue thing in a dark corner. That shit looks real as fuck. Shit made me jump a little, for sure a double-take.

The next day we had our test run. We show up to the side of a large mound with a tunnel bored into the side. It looks like an entrance to a dig site. My CWO sends my team in to investigate as usual. My task is simple: find the contamination. Making my way into the tunnel, I task my two guys to start scanning around.

They found nothing at the entrance, so we probed farther in. Right at that point, I was starting to lose a little light. I immediately got a gut feeling that stopped my ingress. I looked around to see if something might have been watching.

I asked my guys if they found anything, and they had found nothing. Then as I progressed deeper to see if we needed light or not, but something made my spine tingle to my core. I thought, superstitions-there is nothing here, but the hairs on the back of my neck were standing straight up. The feeling of being watched intensified.

There wasn't much in the tunnel, just a few metal drums on the right side of the tunnel. I just scanned those drums and said we didn't find anything. That intense feeling of being watched was accompanied by fear and lasted until we left the tunnel. I did not mention it to my guys, and I don't know if they felt the same.

I don't have an explanation for what I experienced. We were wearing hazmat gear walking down a tunnel with some sensors. Nothing crazy, standard stuff. Although that's the only test run, we were told we failed, meaning... my team failed, and the backup team came back empty-handed. Maybe teams were spooked? No idea. We did like sixteen unique individual simulations and that was the only one that creeped me out.

Ghostly Hikers On Camp Pendleton

I don't know if you've ever heard about the guys that are seen hiking on base on Camp Pendleton at night.

A couple of months after I got here several years ago, someone told me that people have said they've seen Marines hiking in old utilities and packs late at night.

I never really thought about it. Then one night a couple of months ago, I was driving back from a buddy's barracks in San Mateo, and right after the Camp Horno area as you're going towards the air station. I saw three guys hiking along in old style uniforms and packs.

At first I was like, "what the fuck, strange for a Saturday night." When I looked in my mirror to see, sure enough, no one was there. No trace of them, like they were never even there. I try to chalk it up to me being tired, but it's definitely something that gave me chills.

I'm surprised there's not much about Pendleton on this page. This base is spooky as fuck. I swear the Marine Corps/Service can turn any paranormal non-believer into a believer real quick.

Camp Margarita Part I

There were a few things going on in the building we worked in on Camp Margarita. It started as a barracks in the 1950s. There was a ghost there, and it would go around sweeping the halls. It was such a common occurrence we all brushed it off. When you'd see it, you'd be like, "oh, there goes the ghost sweeping the halls."

One time I was out for a walk late at night talking on the phone and I passed the building. I saw all the lights turn on and shadows race past all the windows, then the lights turned back out. It happened over the course of five seconds. I just turned around and walked back home.

Camp Margarita Part II

Another time on Camp Margarita, it was the middle of the day, and this old dude comes in. My corporal and I are like "what's this geezer doing here?" He explained to us that the building we worked in used to be his old barracks before he went to Korea.

He asks if we can take him in the back to see where his old rack was, so my corporal and I take him. Once we're back there, the old guy smiles and starts explaining he slept here and his buddy slept there in this place or that.

After he finishes talking, the dude just fucking evaporates. My corporal and I got immediately freaked out. We chain-smoked the rest of the afternoon asking each other what the fuck just happened.

The Visitor

I had just gotten off my third pump and was back on Pendleton. I woke up in my barracks room and looked from the bed to the other side of the room, only to see another me talking to some type of creature.

The creature's skin was completely green, and it was a few inches taller than me, maybe 6'3" to 6'5". Its whole body was covered in a basic cream-colored shawl. It had sunken cheeks, no nose or ears. It was bald. Its eyes were beady, but no more so than a person with bad genetics. It didn't have any lips, just a slit for a mouth. But in its mouth, it had a bunch of sharp teeth.

I watched the me on the other side of the room, ask it who it was. It told the other me, but I don't remember what it said. Then the other me asked it where it was from, and it said, "Not around here." Any meaning the word "here" conjures in your head applied to the "not here" part. Then other me asked it what it was doing there.

It told other me it was just checking things out. Then it stopped talking to the other me across the room, turned to look at me in bed and hissed, "wake up."

I wake up alone in my room, it's dark, still the middle of the night, and I decide to get some water. As SOON as my feet hit the floor, the lights turn on, and the door and window slam open.

I'm not sure what it was, but I called the guy who lived in that room before me. He was Lakota, if I remember right. But he always said he had a curse put on him when he was a kid, so I think the creature may have been looking for him. I hadn't been in that room for more than a couple of weeks. I sent him a text, and all he said was, "Yeah dude, be careful, there are demons out there."

Something. Is. Wrong.

Okay, so I'm standing duty on the late shift, and I immediately jinx myself by having the thought: "I ain't gonna have to talk to no one tonight, quiet duty."

Then the GySgt, who was the AoD comes on deck at about 0200. He's talking to me, asking how the nights have been, and I'm telling him whatever he wants to hear to get him to fuck off. Finally, he leaves, and I make a note of the Gunny's presence.

At the duty desk area, two monitors show eight cameras across each wing of the barracks and a couple of spots outside. I mention this because I would have seen motion on the camera and heard a notification from the monitors if motion was detected. I finished up the logbook entry and decided I was going to step out to burn one

In the duty hut area, there was a pillar of concrete, probably an excellent 2ftx2ft in dimension. This created a blind spot to a small lounge area; you couldn't see a section of that lounge when at the desk. I had to walk that way to smoke, I walk past the pillar, and my blood goes cold. Something has reached down in my core and pulled at my ancestral alarm instincts. My fight or flight ramping up hardcore.

Something. Is. Wrong.

As all that goes through my head in a split instant, this captain stepped into view. He had to have been posted up behind the pillar in the blind spot. He was a good 6'4, lean, very pale, and when I first noticed him, he had a very stern look on his face. When I popped to attention and started reporting the barracks status, his expression changed to a more relaxed one, his face reset into one with laid-back eyes and a slight grin.

"Easy, their killer, I don't need all that," Is what he said. I asked him: "Sir, it's very late, and I know the OOD is Major [so and so]. Can you provide some ID and a reason for being here?" To which he kind of shook his head, handed me his CAC, and chuckled in response: "you are a thorough one, aren't you?"

I don't remember the name listed, pretty sure the last name was "Jones", but I didn't commit it to memory. He was touring from another post, and I just left it that. He followed me out to the smoke pit, we made small talk about the weather changing, and he left midway through my cigarette.

So, you are probably wondering what makes this so unique of a story. Later that night, maybe around 0330-0400, the OOD comes on deck. I asked him after we exchanged greetings and check-ins if something was up tonight because it's abnormal for the barracks to have so many people on deck at night, surprised he responded: "What do you mean?"

I explained to him that the Gunny came in earlier, then a captain showed up touring, and then he showed up. The OOD was confused because the only other duties that night at the touring post were a LtCol and an SSgt at one building, and a LT and a Sgt at another facility. Whoever it was wasn't supposed to be there or supposedly wasn't on duty

I gave him a description, he made some notes and said he would call back in to confirm if there was a change. Turns out there never was a listed change of duty personnel. I reported it to the OOD. He did whatever from there, I never found out who it was. But there was one thing I didn't report… The one thing I remember clear as day...

The captain's eyes. His eyes were both entirely black. That's what was wrong with him. That's what triggered my brain into panic mode when I saw him. What screamed at me that something wasn't right. I didn't think even to question his eyes; I was caught up in shock, courtesy and fear. I still get chills thinking about it to this day.

The Amityville Room

Not my story but one from my Platoon Sergeant, who lived a few doors down from my room, dubbed "The Amityville Horror Room."

After my Platoon Sergeant's Afghanistan deployment, the former dude in my room started to fall apart. He claimed he could hear voices and shit. Eventually, my SSgt heard wailing through the vents one night, he and some other dudes started to look around to figure out what was going on.

He ended up coming up to the window of my room, looked in, and saw the dude had cut his arms wide open and was sitting in the middle of the room crying.

Luckily the room wasn't locked, so they made entry through the window, managed to stop the bleeding, and transported him to Navy medical. For a long time afterward, blood would ooze up from the tiles, earning the room the name "The Amityville Horror Room."

It wasn't all that surprising to my roommate and I, we'd heard strange noises, and we'd feel stuff brush by our feet in our beds when both of us were alone in the room at night.

It's become familiar enough to where it doesn't even unnerve us that much. We kind of freeze for a second, look at each other and laugh about how the ghost is back.

Bellows

So, when I was stationed in Hawaii, we would go to Bellows a lot for training. I'd always see dark shadows disappearing into the brush while out in the field. I now work up at range control, and I have the night shift: 2000-0600 most nights.

Most commonly, you hear babies crying at night. At first, we thought maybe a mongoose or some animal was making that noise, but after further investigating and research, no explanation came up.

Most of the guys on the night shift sleep and do radio checks with all the units training, but a lot of us have woken up to screaming and loud bangs as if someone was in our ear. You see a lot of shadows moving around out on the range. Some nights you see the motion sensor lights flick on when no one is around.

My buddy said for three weeks straight, he would sit in a chair with his Air Pods in, and he could distinctly hear footsteps behind him when no one was there. He would listen to doors slamming while he was alone in the building.

If you ever go out there at night, you always feel like someone is watching you. I've heard heavy footsteps over in building 700, doors slamming, and loud bangs. Most guys are nervous about going out there at night.

Some guys said they had heard voices over in the MOUT towns. If you ever get a chance, you should explore the old bunkers that they built during WW2. There is a cemetery as well over by building 700.

I've heard babies crying and have seen shadows moving. I haven't heard the kids' voices, but there is a school building with a bunch of mannequins. We'd always go out in the morning to make sure the fences aren't broken, make sure poachers aren't out, and to check in with the units training. We would walk through the MOUTs to make sure everything was in working order. The mannequins would always be outside around the school building, but not in the classroom where they are supposed to be.

Camp Geiger

There is a tale of a little girl that appears in the woods. I saw a small figure running around during my 5k hike, but I just figured I was tired because it was like 0300.

During defense week, I set up security in my fighting hole around midnight. I heard noises in the bush, but I figured it was an animal. 0300 rolled around, and there she was, about five feet away from me. I was so scared I went from brown to pasty white in a second.

I didn't want to call anyone because I didn't think anyone would believe me. So, there I was in a fighting hole staring at this creature, praying that it would go away soon. She vanished into thin air, and I kept quiet about this until I hit the fleet.

I barely knew English back then. Imagine me trying to explain that to an instructor while I'm scared shitless with broken English. But that little girl, she's a typical appearance in Camp Geiger.

Bridgeport

It was about 0100ish, I went to shit. While I was stripping myself to poo, I saw this thing scurry by. It was about the size of deer, but it didn't move like a deer would move. I was too tired, so I didn't think much of it; about five minutes later, I saw something scurry by again. Weird, but I'm trying to finish up my business. Then about 40 yards from me, I see this thing stand up straight out of the brush, and then start running at me.

I started running and as I turned around to look, I see what is chasing me. It had six legs instead of four, so when it stood up, it had four arms. It had the body and legs of a deer, but the arms/hands of a human. This thing had the face of a woman with deer antlers coming out of her head. I kept running for my life, but then I turned around again and it's gone. I didn't sleep the rest of the night.

Norway has some freaky shit too. The polar night seasons get weird. You'd see these figures almost like people with no arms, just walking. You can see them on thermals or plain eyesight. Very ghost-like. Though I think it's the constant darkness fucking with your brain

Bangor, WA

So, I was originally security forces for the USMC in Bangor, WA and I worked the waterfront for a little over 2.5 years. That post isn't stood anymore to my knowledge, I'm not positive, I'm not stationed there anymore.

We'd have shadow figures when I was a junior constantly at the north end of the waterfront, randomly at night creeping around on the trestles. There was an entity people called the JIG, Jawless

Indian Girl, that would haunt the main road we made moves on. Screams late at night at certain piers and supposedly a haunted painting.

We'd randomly see these tall things; I mean pretty tall too, around 8-11' feet roughly. You only see them at night time, never when foggy. Super skinny beings and they could move pretty quick. We were standing post one time, and my senior glanced to check the cameras that covered 360° of our post. I saw one at the end of the pier, near the main road, probably 125-150 yards away. It came down the trestle, ran quickly towards our post, and disappeared maybe 10 yards before coming to the door.

Later that night, we'd heard something banging loudly on the front door. You would open the front door and as soon as the front door opened, the rear door would get a bang on it. Cameras picked up no one, and the post 25 yards away, didn't even hear or see anything.

As for the JIG, I never had a solid encounter seeing her with my own eyes. But I was on watch one night and on my rest cycle. I was sleeping in pretty big berthing area, all to myself. I turned off the lights and racked out; I woke up around 0200-0300 to the red lights on and goosebumps. I got up to turn off the lights and heard tiny footsteps behind me. Spooked, I bolted to the watch room where the other person was at. Footsteps followed me until getting into the main room. It was just a creepy feeling.

The screams I never personally heard, but my seniors heard them when they worked at Bangor as boots. They were building a pier, and the only way to get there was by boat. They experienced blood-curdling screams happening in the middle of the night out there. The base police would get phone calls from that specific pier same time frame, but no one would be on the other end.

There is a picture rumored to have the JIG appear in and out of it. It's a painting of the Northwestern waterfront, the general area. According to some, she would appear in the painting in the woods on the painting. Other days she wouldn't.

Some shadows or (beings) taunted post standers on the area's northern edge. They appeared mid-morning, early afternoon in the bushes, maybe 50 yards from the post. Happened to me and a buddy, maybe a 4.5' x 2-3' blob. Made a shallow, growling-type sound, and slowly moved back into the woods. We were curious and started following it and took the dirt road to the west of the woods. It slowly was moving further down parallel to the road but also most into the woods. We started walking into the woods themselves, following it. We both noticed no more sounds from the birds or nature. We quickly got back on the road, went condition one each, and walked back to post. I had a very bad feeling the rest of the night and was pretty sick the rest of the day from it, i.e., throwing up, headaches.

Finally, I was told a story before I arrived at Bangor: when my team leader was there, someone fucked up and had to run back to the quarters. My team leader then followed behind in a bearcat. As they were running, the dude who fucked up and my team leader both saw something matching their jog in the woods to their left, the western part before the road wraps around. My team leader ordered the guy to get in the bearcat, and they drove back. Later on, if you asked separately, they would tell you the same thing. They described it as a large (maybe furry?) creature matching their speed but on all fours. Very big, bigger than a black bear, and much bigger than the blacktail deer that live out there.

The Shuffler Of Camp Devil Dog

I was at ITB in December 2018. Our last training event before we got sent home for Christmas recruiting duty was defense week. We would go out to Camp Devil Dog, stage our main packs at the CoC, and each platoon split up to set up a patrol base. My buddy and I got our spot and dug in. We weren't going to be patrolling that night, so we each decided to take turns on watch two hours at a time.

At about 0200ish, I started hearing movement behind our line and got a little spooked. But I figured it was just one of the instructors checking if kids were awake or not. I'm looking back over my right shoulder and can't make anything out with my NVG. But that night the moonlight was bright and I could see with my naked eye too.

I see a figure standing directly behind the fighting hole next to us, leaning in. I can't see it with my naked eye, but I can see it with my

NVG clearer now that I'm focused on it. It doesn't move for a while, and I figure maybe it's just a bent-over tree or something. I could see IR light movement from the adjacent hole, so I knew the guy in that hole was awake and looking around.

Just as I was about to turn back to the front, this figure straightens up, and I realize it is tall as hell. This thing turns its body toward me, and I start panicking. It slowly begins to shuffle, walking around the hole behind me, past mine, into the tree line ahead of me.

I'm shitting bricks, and for the rest of my watch, I'm hyper-focused scanning the tree line looking for anything. But not too long after it disappeared, my buddy starts screaming from where he's slumped in the hole: "I can't breathe, I can't breathe, I can't breathe!" I yank him up by the flak, his eyes open, and he looks at me. When I let go, he slumps back down and falls asleep again. When I woke him up for his watch, he didn't remember screaming. It gives me goosebumps to think about it to this day.

My memory of it is pretty shaky, but whatever it was black, and the proportions of the limbs were weird. The arms and legs seemed too long for its torso. The only other thing I can remember about it was how it moved, the way it moved was extremely awkward. When I say "shuffled," I mean it. It slid its feet along the ground instead of fully picking them up.

Range 215

I was out there with 3/8 Lima on range 215 for AFX, and we had occupied a building as our OP. My watch shift was from 0300-0400. Some people call that the devil's hour, so the whole time leading up to that, that's all I could think about. I wake up at around 0245 to get dressed and get started.

Once I settled into my watch, I immediately started hearing footsteps upstairs. Yet the whole team was sleeping on the bottom floor. Doors began to open and close on their own, and there was little to no wind during this time. I didn't see anything, but there was this one door. This one door would slam harder than all the rest. It freaked me out so bad I didn't leave my sleeping bag.

I woke up my RO, who was sleeping right next to me, and asked him if he could hear the same shit. He did and he got spooked too, as he had watch right after me. We didn't leave the corner of this room we were sleeping in the whole night.

Camp Pendleton Navy Hospital

One October night back in 2018, my friends and I were stationed at Camp Pendleton. My one friend had just bought a Ouija board, so we made the ethical decision to (of course) go to the old abandoned Naval Hospital and see if we can "talk to some ghosts" over there (which I am fully aware is the smartest idea in the whole world).

We get there, parking at Wounded Warriors Clinic to not bring attention to PMO or anyone else. We walk over and look around. The Naval Hospital itself was locked tight. I being the resident wimp of the group, was ready to bail. Then mysteriously, we see one door open, into the boiler room. I swear we checked the Naval Hospital twice and saw no entries open until we were about to leave.

It was pitch dark in the boiler room itself. There were two parts to the room, the entry before the boilers and a space behind the boilers themselves. We went to the second space behind the boilers and close the door behind us. Equipped with flashlights, a candle, and a Ouija board. We begin, and at first, everything is normal.

We are trying to stay quiet, so we can listen to any possible PMO come in and got down to business. We begin asking questions and in response we got a "JR" who died there, etc., etc.

Then, as we asked if he was a good or evil spirit, the handpiece was inching to spelling out "bad." We heard the door (we closed behind us) slam open and footsteps walk into the room. So, I'm like, cool, we've been caught. We leave to go to the entryway to meet what we believed would be the cops waiting for us. But there was no one and nothing to be seen, just the door wide open.

Shadow People In The Hills

During the workup to deployment, our Scout Sniper platoon was tasked to assist some unit test their ground sensors and GBOSS. Our platoon was broken up into three teams, and our mission was to insert, set up an OP, and observe the MOUT town the guys were set up in to see if they would detect us or if we could complete a 48HR mission without being compromised.

Most of our platoons HOGs were gone at this time as they were at advanced schools to get more training before we headed off to 29 Palms. For this mission, one of our more senior PIGs was the team leader, but this guy didn't give a fuck about anything, so our plan was garbage from the start.

We insert at around 2200 and instantly got lost as we had almost no route plan. Around 0200, we decided to try and go through a draw between two hills and then up the side of one to set up. By 0300, we stop, and the TL and our point man go off to do a leader's recon to find a suitable hide. I'm left-back because I'm the RO and my friend with me is the ARO. We're sitting on the side of the hill and can see into the valley and the mountain across from us.

Since we're in a "security posture," I'm looking through my NVGs to waste time, and I see "them." On the hillside opposite us, I can see two completely black human silhouettes moving down the hill and in our direction. I figure since I've been up all day and night, I am hallucinating or something, so I look away for a while and try to regain some focus.

When I look back, they're still there and standing still. I kept watching them for about 15-20 minutes, and they remained stationary and seemingly looking back at my friend and I.

Eventually, the TL returned, and we set in, but I couldn't sleep much because of the experience. I thought I had a hallucination and never brought it up. Fast forward, one night a couple of my friends and I were drinking, and my friend who was with me told the same story from his perspective, almost exactly as I experienced it and remembered it.

The only way I can describe what I saw was that they were completely black human silhouettes. It was around 0200-0300 in late winter so it was very dark out, but they were the darkest things I could see through my NVGs. The valley/draw between the two hills was almost pitch black, but the two figures I saw were as darker while making their way down the mountain.

The only other thing I could add is that as I'd focus on them, the one on the left would seem to lose its definite human outline and appear to grow taller, while the one on the right would seem to shrink down to a shorter figure if I focused on it. When looking at both, they would seem to be approximately the same height.

After seeing where the other two teams set up, it couldn't have been them. It turns out we got so lost we were alone and took so long to get into our OP, the other two teams were set in long before we did. With all the history of Pendleton, I wouldn't be surprised if there's something out there. Guess I'll never know.

Ghost Tanks

So I want to start this off by saying this was my 2nd or 3rd month in the Jacksonville, NC area. I had just been stationed on MCAS New River, but I wanted to explore Lejeune because I knew I would have to go there from time to time to perform my duties and such. So one night around midnight, I get in my car and head over to Lejeune and drive around exploring and learning my way around the base.

At around 0300, I decided to head back to my barracks and I plug it into my GPS. Long story short, I get lost and I end up on a long road down towards one of the base's decommissioned gates (way back near Hubert). If you've spent any time in the Onslow area, you know that the wee hours of the morning can get pretty foggy and it creates an overall uneasy feeling.

I realize my mistake, turn around, and start heading back the way I came. As I am driving back, my car starts to jump and shake (I guessed that one of the artillery battalions was running a night op close by). I keep going down this road and it's lined by street lights maybe 100 ft or more apart, illuminating the street through the fog just enough. All of a sudden, it feels like I was on a draw bridge.

I shit you not three tanks (vintage-looking, maybe Vietnam era) come rolling from the tree line on the right about 300 feet away from me. They travel across the road and into the tree line on the other side of the road. They had men manning the turrets and everything. I could only make out the men from the shoulders up, but they weren't wearing our modern kevlar helmets. Instead it looked like they had old GI helmets with no covers on from the way the streetlights reflected off the tops.

After they passed, I immediately thought I might've accidentally ventured into a restricted part of the base, like a range or something. But when I got to where they crossed, there were no signs of them! No muddy track marks, and both tree lines were super dense. You couldn't even fit a squad through there without at least hacking a few saplings down. I don't know what I saw, but those tanks and Soldiers looked like they were straight out of Vietnam.

MCRD San Diego

Recruiter school on MCRD San Diego is haunted as fuck. I, another dude, and SNCO are on duty because fuck the students. When we got the brief, they said the school was haunted. The instructors themselves have seen freaky shit and everything. Footsteps down the halls, yelling, doors opening and closing, lights coming on when they've been shut off, the works.

So, while we are on duty, we have to cut off all the lights beside the lower deck. We go upstairs, shut off every single light in the classrooms, and head outside to get some pizza across the street. When we came back out, all the lights upstairs were back on.

We asked the SNCO if he went upstairs, and he's like, "nope!" So we go upstairs and check it out. Well, when we get upstairs and shut off all the lights again, we start hearing loud ass footsteps coming up the stairs that we came up. But when we ran to look, no one was there.

White Lights At 29 Palms

3rd LAR, 29 Palms. Near the end of 2014, I was out in the field. The first night of the ITX, the vehicles halt, and we set into a screen line. We're getting ready to bed down for the night, but we haven't dismounted.

I was an IAR gunner at the time, so I was popped out of the back hatch, and next to me standing out of the other hatch was my team leader. Behind us we begin to hear coyotes going about their business.

I flip my NVG up to clean my glasses and when I put them back on, I see four white lights in the distance. I think to myself, "what're those idiots doing out there? They're giving themselves away!" All of a sudden, those four lights fly up into the sky, faster than anything I'd seen in my life.

I asked my TL if he saw that, and he wasn't paying attention to our rear, so he didn't catch it and asked me what it was. Not wanting to sound stupid, I said that someone flashed their lights at us. But I don't believe for a minute that's what it was. Whatever it was, I don't think it was a drone, aircraft, or anything manmade.

Last Man

MCRD Parris Island, I was 1st BN, A Co., this was 2006. We were doing A-Line and basic warrior tasks out at Paige Field. I was the last recruit in line to do the night infiltration course. It was the latter end of twilight, almost full-blown night. A random DI wearing old woodland BDUs came out of the tree line with a male recruit wearing the current digital uniform.

I went to give him the greeting of the day, but before I could speak, he snapped, "Don't fucking look at me." He orders the other recruit to stick with me. We never exchanged names and just went along with it because I was a scared private. But when we started walking away, I looked behind me, and this DI fucking VANISHED into thin air. I was like, where the fuck did he go? This "kid" responded, "oh yeah, he does that sometimes."

We negotiate this course. When we reached the end, the DIs were taking accountability. As I turned to look at the other recruit to say, "we fuckin' did it" and he was gone!

A DI approached me and asked me to ID myself. All he said was, "yeah! This is the LAST ONE." Falling back in with my Platoon, I told them I'd been with another recruit. A group of them told me, "Nah, man. You were the last one." I was in shock. I had full blown conversations with this "kid." I have no explanation to this day for what it was.

BTW, The Barracks Are Haunted

In the third phase at Parris Island, we were all standing Fire Watch. It was the 0200 shift. I was at the front of the Squad Bay near the head door by the DI Hut. I start hearing a metallic, rhythmic clinking. I walk into the showers to investigate. At first, I thought it was the old steam pipes in the building.

As I got to the rain room (big shower room), the sound stopped. I turned around to walk out. The sound resumed again; this time loud as fuck. I step back into the shower; I see all of the washers behind the faucet knobs bouncing in unison against the walls. Just, "clink-clink-clink-clink." I think I'm tripping. I walk out to get my buddy. He thinks I'm fucking around. The sound resumes, and I lead him back into the showers where he sees the same thing I did.

We walk out of the showers, and the oncoming shift shows up. We tell them what's up. Of course, they are skeptical, because "it's 3rd Phase guys, it's too silly for shit like this." The sound at that exact moment picked back up.

One of the guys on the oncoming shift goes in, and he comes sprinting out. The final skeptic was an atheist. He goes in, and he comes out; his eyes are bloodshot. He's like, "I thought you guys were fucking with me, but there is absolutely no scientific explanation for what the FUCK IS GOING ON IN THERE."

The following day, I walked in during general clean-up. I went to grab one of the washers behind the faucet knobs. It was fastened solid to the wall.

Later that night, during Senior Drill Instructor time, unprovoked he looked up at all of us and said, "oh yeah, by the way, the Barracks ARE haunted."

FOREIGN MILITARIES

If it's not foreign, it's boring…

CANADIAN ARMED FORCES

Dads Bigfoot Story

The following is a story from my dad. He's a former paratrooper, Senior NCO, and 20+ year police officer. He's a no-BS hard charger.

During the mid-70's, on a winter exercise on the west coast of Canada, his platoon was set up for a night ambush on the OPFOR. The night was a bright, full moon night with a light coat of fresh snow.

While lying in position, an overwhelming stink of rotten meat and wet dog wafts over them. Then along a nearby tree line just off the X, they see a hulking lone figure go speed walking by. Quick pace, covering a reasonable distance fast, but not running.

Initially they thought it was the company commander, who stood at 6'8", getting into a position to watch the ambush unfold. Post ambush, they go over to where they saw the figure. The company commander joined them, and he came nowhere near the height as the figure did when compared to the trees. When comparing the stride and speed of the figure, the commander couldn't match the speed or the gait of what the platoon witnessed. Even more telling: upon searching the area where they all witnessed the figure, they discovered in the fresh snow massive, bare footprints.

My dad's platoon was particular about what they saw that night. They saw bigfoot.

Wainwright Training Center

Wainwright Training Center, Alberta, Canada. We do probably 90% of our training there, and there are all kinds of stories of unknown dismounts, "Sasquatch," wendigo sightings, and shadow figures on thermals. After clearance patrols or investigations into these sightings, usually nothing turns up.

Anyways, we were midway through Exercise Maple Resolve a few years back getting some rest for a few days in a cop of trees. We were hearing weird shit the entire time: walking around our ten-man tents at 0300, bizarre animal noises that don't sound like any animal you've ever heard, and guys claimed they heard a woman crying in the night.

That same week one night I get woken up violently from a slap on my legs. Felt like a log was dropped on them in the tent. I spring up instantly scared shitless, and everyone is still racked; I didn't hear anyone rustling around. I asked the lads the next day, and two days prior my boy had woken up in the middle of the night to someone or something grabbing him in his sleeping bag and everyone was asleep. I told myself it was just the dudes fucking with us but it still weirds me out thinking about it!

Meaford Mary I

Canadian Armed Forces. February 9th, 2021- 4 CDTC Meaford, 0300, on defensive exercise, manning the C6. I'm scanning my arcs with the NVGs when I hear laughing.

Look in the direction of the laughter and see a young lady in a white dress standing in the woods on my right arc. I rub my eyes, and she was gone, so I chalk it up to being sleep fucked.

Find out later that some of the other guys experienced the same thing. I asked the staff if it was part of an OPFOR joke, they replied, "Nope, that was Meaford Mary checking the lines."

Two days later, I'm doing a night recce against the OPFOR base camp. I see a figure standing between me and the lights, so I slowly get low. OPFOR sees another guy doing the cloverleaf, so all hell breaks loose. I hear a para flare go up, and suddenly the figure was gone…Meaford Mary must've been sweet on me or something.

Nobody has a clue who Mary is. I've heard some guys speculate that it's the ghost of a local from the town nearby, but there's no definitive backstory. I know several people, some of whom have trained Meaford years before me, who have encountered Meaford Mary.

CFB Petawawa

Mattawa Plains, CFB Petawawa. My buddy and I were assigned as OPFOR for a Section Commander Course, and we both swear there were Skinwalkers in the forest with us. Coincidentally, the area we were in is aptly named "Skinwalker Forest." We were supposed to be get spotted (on purpose) by the course students, so we moved with white lights on. It was raining, and even with white light, it killed our visibility.

We started seeing large shadows (7+ ft tall) running through the woods. I couldn't get a clear glimpse as they were running really fast. We saw the shadows a couple of times while we were static. I'd ballpark that the shadows maintained ~50m distance from us when we saw them. We thought it should have been the course students/instructors. I called their NCOIC to ask if he was nearby, he replied they were crashing at the bivouac 2km away from us.

The end of the phase came, so we packed up and headed towards the road for our ride back to camp. We were smoking and joking on our way over, and both of us caught a glimpse of what looked like Skinwalker/Wendigo standing on the trail before darting back into the woods. We both swore it looked like the stereotypical depiction of the Wendigo. Safe to say, I didn't sleep that night. To this day, I refuse to go into the woods alone.

Canadian Navy '67

So, this is a story I learned from my uncle. Not exactly the longest or scariest, though I figured it might pique someone's interest, I'll try my best to retell it.

Back in his hay day, my uncle was in the Royal Canadian Navy, working in a certain Atlantic province. He had made a few good friends, one of whom was a diver. One night, said diver friend decided to let him in on a bit of story.

In October of '67, the diver friend was stationed around Shelburne, Nova Scotia, when they were put on a sudden deployment. They were put aboard a destroyer and were sent out with the Canadian Coast Guard and, if I recall correctly, even an American vessel.

About two or three days into this voyage and my uncle's diver friend is told to prepare to go into the water. So, a few minutes later, he's off into the waters. Everything's pitch black down there, and suddenly he sees this yellow light.

As he gets closer and catches a better look, it becomes clear it's not a light but rather a craft of some sort. It allegedly seemed to be resting on the bottom, or in some distress, with "entities" of some sort floating around it. Diver friend is down there for a few good minutes, and as he's going up, he sees another amber light coming into view but has to leave the waters before he can get a good look.

While he told my uncle he could neither confirm nor deny what he saw, he believed it was some USO/UFO. Usually, I'd believe it to be some tall tale sailors tell one another, but there's one thing that always irked me about it. The date that my uncle's diver friend claims this occurred, was only a few days after the alleged UFO Crash in Shag Harbor, Nova Scotia.

RTOs And UFOs

I was sitting on radio watch, and a reservist at another grid calls the CP with "contact NO DUFF UFO IVO (grid ref)." The CP advises calling station to find a replacement for a radio watch, and that sleep deprivation causes hallucinations.

While listening to this play out (and having a minor chuckle about it), the sky starts getting brighter. I thought it was a para flare, but as I look outside… this glowing mass cuts overhead about 300ft up and then fucks off into the sky. No sound, light for maybe 10 seconds, then nothing. It looked like an arrowhead, but the light made it hard to distinguish features.

In 2017, we were doing a bigger exercise on the prairies of Alberta. Three of us were walking though the tent lines and a giant arrowhead flies overhead. This time no light, it buzzed us overhead, and it had metallic features before vanishing. We initially thought it was part of the "open skies treaty," but it made no sense for an aircraft to be that low, let alone make no sound as it passed over.

Little Demons

Canadian Army here. Did my Infantry DP1 (battle school) a few years ago in CFB Shilo, universally known as a place devoid of joy and comfort. One of the last parts of the course is the defensive warfare portion: which is just over a week of digging trenches, sending out patrols, following track plans, improving trenches, resisting attacks, and hating your life.

As I'm sure is the same in other countries battle schools, you don't get a lot to eat, get almost no sleep, and get a ton of work. On the last night, when running on five days of no rest, we got attacked in the middle of the night, and were called to stand to.

There was a big attack by OPFOR and they cleared off after about 45 minutes of throwing arty sims and shooting at us. At the end of the attack, I sat there smiling, feeling incredibly glad the defensive was only going to last a few more hours, and after that I could sleep.

The context for this next bit: My fire team partner was a dude from the RWR whose mascot was a little black devil. They called themselves "the little black devils," and had t-shirts with the name, etc. So I was seeing and hearing a lot about little black devils.

So back to the trench: I look over at the trench to my left, about 20 meters away, and I see a little black devil (one foot tall maybe) running in between the trenches, cackling and peering in. A little black man (not racially black but just colored black) with big teeth, big hands, big red eyes, and about a foot tall; moving really fast, laughing, and babbling nonsense.

The cheeky little bastard runs right up to my trench, muttering and cackling. He peeks his head over the side to look at me, and runs off. As I said, I assume being up for five days is getting to me, and I write it off as sleep deprivation.

I finish the last patrol, head back to our patrol hide, and we finally get the order to rack out. Best sleep of my life. I wake up and start talking to my section about how fucking awful the defensive was and how sleep fucked everyone got.

I bring up my black devil hallucination, and the air immediately changes in the section. Two other guys around me also saw the exact little black devil thing at the same time I did. I still have no idea what happened. Either a coincidence, group hallucination, or Shilo may be worse than we thought.

The Garrison

Canadian Army officer here. I work in a garrison that's been in service since before WW2. In one of the old hangars (now demolished, there used to be airplanes there), we had our mess (the bar where we could grab a drink). In the officer mess, there was a bible, an ancient bible that nobody knew exactly where it came from. Everyone that has worked around that bible has heard or seen weird shit.

Every once in a while, we would find this old bible thrown around in a complete mess. The Bible next to two newer condition bibles in a locked glass display. We found this super weird, but there's a civilian airport next to our base, so we thought maybe the vibration or airplanes caused this. We even changed the camera's direction to try to catch if someone was messing with the bible, but we never saw anything.

Then one day, we had to do some renovations, and there were these huge cylindrical stands. They were very, very heavy, and for a reason I don't remember, we left the three bibles on the top of one of the stands. The day after the cylinders were discovered as if they were thrown across the room, and the bibles were thrown not far from where the cylinder fell.
In another occurrence, two female NCOs were working near the

stand where the bibles were. The floor was made in a kind of old wood/plastic which, with our boots, made it very easy to know whenever someone was coming. The two NCOs (master corporal and a corporal) were in different rooms.

The master corporal was focused working when she suddenly heard boots running right to her, close to the door entrance. She didn't see anything because of course that building was ancient and never had great light. She turned super-fast and yelled to the corporal if it was her that just passed next to her. The corporal yelled in the other room that it wasn't her. No need to say they left the building fast.

There's been a lot of occurrences like that. Even a captain refused to touch the display that held the bibles and made privates move it for him. The building was demolished maybe two years ago, and we never heard what happened to that devilish book.

Meaford Mary II

So back in late 2018 and late November, I was tasked with playing OPFOR for infantry courses being run. We all had heard the stories of "blue eyes" and how she screams from inside the forest near the urban ops range.

One night we were in the basement of this three-story house, and we were all trying to get some sleep. That night we all had woken up to the sound of footsteps from upstairs on the main floor. We also heard what sounded like a full-blown conversation between a female and some other thing.

The steps went down to the basement, suddenly stopped, and the entire air was just super still. We all had this feeling that something nasty was going to come around the corner. The steps went back upstairs, and that was that.

We asked the course staff if they were in the building, and no one was there but us that night. I've heard countless stories and even seen what looked like someone walking through the trees in my NVGs during the course.
I don't know if most people know this about Meaford, but it was old farmland bought out years ago. There's even a tombstone with this

cage over where they would bury a body. No one's why it's there

No one knows who Mary is and there is a lot of mystery about who she is. I believe that people's misery or depression or anything tragic can attract "not very good things" to areas. Before I got to Meaford, there were many suicides months before I arrived. She could be many things, but she is there now

One guy I knew was on the same course, in the same urban ops area. He and a few guys were sitting at the 84mm dugout, and for the entire night he was there, he kept hearing this female voice giving him orders and telling him to leave his post.

Another story I heard is the screaming that comes out of the forest. I even spoke to this super intense warrant talk about this back trail near the urban ops area, that he will not go down for reasons he did not disclose.

Meaford Mary III

This story takes place on the Meaford Tank Range in Meaford, Ontario (between Collingwood and Owen Sound). On the northeast tip of the peninsula, there are many old stone ruins that the Army Reserve uses for training. There are old foundations everywhere as a community of farmers used to live there. Many ghost stories have come up from around the area, and here is mine.

On my introductory training course, we were told about a little girl's ghost on the east coast of the peninsula. The story is that the little girl had been out picking flowers, as she usually did before dinner when her mother called. Her house and that area of the base are all forest and sit on top of a vast cliff edge that goes down into Georgian Bay.

The little girls' mom called, and she came running, but what she didn't see was the old boarded-up well that her parents always warned her about. She fell into the well and was there for a good while. As she was eight years old and could swim, it took a long time for her to succumb to hypothermia and drown in the well. She screamed for help the whole time. A gravestone still sits outside between the house and the well. I have personally seen it.

Back to the ghost story: two years ago, I was on patrol with my section commander and three other guys. We were doing a reconnaissance patrol of a road. It was mid-August, about 0300hrs in the morning. We had reports from the base command that new artillery gunners might have hit an old road through that part of the woods. Command wanted to know if we could still use the road and to confirm any damage.

As we began our movement along the road, we could see something moving in the woods. There was a bit of white glow, and we all could feel that we were being watched. We all wanted out of there. The air turned like ice, and our hair stood on end.

Our stomachs dropped to our feet when we heard "help me...please help me" from a little girl's voice far off in the distance. We all knew we heard it and wanted to help, but our section commander said: "No, that is the way to the old well. Lots of troops have fallen into that well. Lucky none have died yet, but anyone who has gone after the little girl has fallen into the well."

Soon after this, we realized we lost one of our troops on patrol. We went back to find him headed right to the well. "I could hear a little girl moaning for help, and I lost track of you guys after I stopped to listen," he said. We grabbed him and left the area.

About a year later, on patrol, and at about the same time at night as before; I could see what I thought to be a little girl in an old Victorian style nightgown in the woods about 150m away. This time I saw her through IR night vision goggles. No voice accompanied the apparition, only her and the same creepy feeling. The air once again turned cold, and the hair on my neck stood on end until she walked out of sight.

CFB Petawawa

So young Pvt (myself) gets put on the late-night duty desk watch. The unit is empty, and I start doing lock up. I hear footsteps in random hallways even though the other private is manning the phone, everyone is gone, and we are alone.

I walk through the unit memorial hallway headed to the washroom.

As I walk past pictures of our fallen, I feel as though someone is breathing down my neck. As I entered the washroom fucking every faucet deployed as if on que as soon as I walked in. I sprinted back to the desk and then went for a smoke.

To further the weirdness in this building, a good friend of mine volunteered for duty while others were on leave. He slept in a platoon office on a random camp cot. In the middle of the night, he felt his foot being grabbed and pulled off the cot. His partner was passed out at the duty deck, and they were all alone in the building.

Camp Aldershot Part I

In Camp Aldershot, Nova Scotia, Canada. I was in the field during basic training when my section and I were on a late-night recce. We were deep in the woods and stopped for a listening halt. After a few minutes, we stepped off again.

I saw my section get up and start moving down the trail, so I followed. I knew I was following them because I could see their silhouettes bobbing. It literally looked like five guys in CADPAT, like I was sure they were my section members. I could still see the cat eyes on the back of their helmets.

I heard a voice behind me say, "where are you going?". I turned around to see my section was walking in the opposite direction. And when I looked back to see what I initially thought was my section, there was nobody there. Maybe it was sleep deprivation, but it never sat right with me.

Camp Aldershot Part II

While on the trench line, I was watching for OPFOR when I saw five or six bright blue lights shoot up into the sky, one after another. They shot up and then just hovered in place, lighting up the area around me. At first I thought they were our Para-flares, but I remembered that they are supposed to be bright white.

Nobody called a stand too, and after hovering for a short amount of time, they just disappeared. They didn't fly away or fall back down, just blink and they are gone! The lights had vanished and the area around me was dark again. In the morning, I asked if anyone else had seen them, and nobody did. Maybe I was just sleep fucked, but it still is spooky in my opinion.

Canadian Forest

I was a Canadian Cadet at a company level FTX at CFB Gagetown. I woke up in the dead of night; my tent was very far away from any other tent; I am in a bit of nook between two patches of forest.

I woke up scared shitless, but I got to pee. I do my business, and I look up in the woods when I'm done. It goes all quiet, and there's just enough light from the moon that I see a pair of antlers and dark eyes, maybe five to six feet in the air.

No other noises, except the occasional artillery shell in the distance. Everything was quiet. No wind. No branches or birds. I don't know what it was, but nothing scared me more. It was eerie. Didn't seem like a deer at all. I slowly backed up when back into my tent. I couldn't sleep all night.

Later that night, I had to go again. This time I woke my buddy up. We walk over this time to the porta johns down the road near our biv site. In the woods, we hear a loud crack and groan. Nothing I heard before, and I've heard yells and other odd stuff from the woods. Freaked out, we decide to go back to the tent—we haven't spoken a word about it since.

Comparing Notes

I was on a course (Canadian Army) when I came across some of our guys "shooting the shit" with some American Soldiers from Fort Drum and Fort Lewis on our course.

The Americans were exchanging Sasquatch stories with guys from the Canadian Infantry out of Alberta. I laughed at first, but they were being serious, and the stories they were sharing were very similar - especially about the smell.

212

The Canadian guys said when they were out in the field near the Rockies, they would hear them (heavy steps) but never see them. Once in a while, this stench would come out of nowhere, and they'd listen to strange "whoops and howls" that came from the forest.

The one American story I recall was this American out of Fort Lewis. He was on watch inside a fenced-off area within the training area (which sounded like how an ammo store looks). He would see these tall things pop out of the distant tree line and sometimes approach the first-line defense. He told the story as if it were a common experience that Soldiers had out there. He and his friends also talked about a horrible stench that would come out of nowhere and disappear just as quick.

The point I am trying to make is the stories between the Canadians and Americans were eerily similar. These guys believed what they were saying. It was almost like they were comparing notes and having a laugh about it.

Canadian Navy Experiences

I'm an air controller in the Canadian Navy. When our aircraft are far away, we use HF to check in with them. In the meantime, we have to sit there and listen. When you're sitting there, you hear things that sound an awful lot like language, but the cadence and rhythm of it doesn't sound like any language you would expect to hear in Atlantic.

Sometimes you'll hear low, distorted voices that seem to be speaking random words without any correlation. It could be just a long-range pickup from stations way away, but sometimes it sounds otherworldly. I've heard some weird-ass shit for sure. Apparently, transmissions can get stuck, go out and come back years later.

I've got a ghost story from a destroyer too.
I've got a ghost story from a destroyer, the Athabaskan. On the Athabaskan, before it got decommissioned, I was on duty one night and I was the only one staying in my mess on the ship that night.

About halfway through my off-watch, I heard footsteps walking around the mess and curtains opening. I got up to have a look around, and it was still just me in the mess. The footsteps stopped when I got out of my rack and then started again when I got back in. That was creepy as hell.

I was just a new sailor at the time, but I guess other guys have walked into the mess on duty and seen an old sailor smoking a pipe. They'd talk to him, and then he'd disappear. The old ships are always creepy, it seems.

I also heard and saw three people marching at an ex-naval base one night. Two other guys and I heard someone calling drill and turned to look (I was on a long straight road, lit by street lamps) and saw a small division of sailors in older dress uniforms. The voice sounded British, and there hadn't been British sailors there since the war. We looked at each other, then back, but the sailors were gone. There's nowhere they could've turned that we wouldn't have seen them, and when we went to look, we found no trace of them. We ran the rest of the way back to the blocks. It was pretty creepy.

We've encountered other strange things, peculiar things. Like a contact will show up on the air radar, rip about 15 miles in five seconds, stop, rip off somewhere else, and then crazy altitude changes at speeds way too fast for an aircraft to do. Sometimes we pick stuff up that reads out at 200,000 feet, and then it will disappear again. One night we were at sea, and a flying object approached us. It was night and no one could tell what it was. Just a light on a stick was how it was described. The ocean holds a lot of secrets.

The Tunnel

Not my story but from a buddy who didn't believe in spirits/ghosts or whatever you want to call them.

It was on his BMQ at an armory. A little history: the armory in question has all these tunnels connected into the basement that was at one point accessible from the junior ranks mess. The building in question is so old it was once a fort. I'm purposefully vague on names and locations for obvious reasons. That's about as much as I can tell you.

Many years ago, there was a problem troop, who was just constantly not switched on, never really fully there. One day, problem troop manages to get himself a standard-issue hi-power and is down in these tunnels, causing problems. A sergeant goes down there to confront him, yelling at him, trying to get him to put the gun down, and the problem troop shoots the sergeant in the chest. The sergeant screamed in agony for quite some time before the problem troop shot him and then himself.

My buddy and his fire team partner are walking around on a fire watch when they both hear running footsteps behind them. They turn around, and the sergeant is full sprinting at them. Once they turned around and begin running themselves, the sergeant started screaming. The screams sounded like a man in agony. They brought this story to the chaplain as they were quite disturbed when he shared this info with him.

AUSTRALIAN ARMED FORCES

The Thing

So Australian Army, I was doing a training exercise in the Northern Territory of Australia. It was a section worth of men, so about nine men. We were sleeping in two positions only about five meters apart. Everyone had racked out and gone to sleep. At about 0300 I heard someone yelling, "NO! NO!" I had no idea who was crying. I shouted out and asked if they were alright, no response. The yelling continued, "NO!"

I sat up in my sleeping bag and looked over at my two other mates, who had also sat up, and we all looked at each other like, "what the fuck." I got out of my sleeping bag and started to walk towards where the other group was sleeping. That's when I saw this thing. It was this tall, slender figure. I couldn't make out a face or any particular detail of it—just a shadow standing there over the top of one of my mates. It stood about six feet tall. It was a long, slender/skinny build. Long forearms. Dark shadow-like figure. Didn't appear to be wearing any clothes, just a shadow

I saw its head look up towards me, and then the only way I can describe it is that it "melted" down onto all fours. It didn't hunch over or bend down. It just collapsed on itself, and then it was on all fours. This thing then crawled off.

I looked at the other two that had woken up simultaneously as me, and we all ran over to where it was standing. There was no sign of anything being there, and the asleep guys hadn't even been woken up. We had to shake them to wake them up. They were still numb out cold. They didn't hear any yelling or anything happening. The thing disappeared, not a trace.

BRITISH ARMED FORCES

Salisbury Plain

During an exercise at Salisbury Plain Training Area in the UK last year, I was dropped off in the dead of night at an abandoned farm with some kit and was asked to set up before the HQ element of our group arrived.

The farm was empty, just made up of old barns and derelict buildings. I found an old farmhouse and started to set up, it was a little creepy there, but I just got on with my task.

It wasn't long before the creepy feeling turned into dread; I sensed something was in there with me just watching. There was one corner of the room that had my constant interest. Although I could barely see, I was convinced something was there, even if it was just an animal or something.

I was in full conversation with my wife back home via text message, and I decided to take a picture to show her our shelter for the night, not expecting to capture what appeared to be a figure lurking in the corner. I spent the rest of the night outside making roll-up cigarettes.

The Onlooker

May 2017 Imber Village, Salisbury Plain. We were finishing an offensive operation and changing into the defense. We had our warrior AFV's and HMMVS in a ring of steel around the houses we occupied and were set in for the remainder of the evening until the OPFOR shook themselves back out (they had recce screens around the village).

We were taking turns on roaming watch, one to two men dependent on how you wanted to skin it on your rotation. A buddy and I were walking around the village shooting the shit and sharing a few clouds of smoke when we sat on a wall, and I looked up to a top floor window.

For those that don't know the houses, there is only one doorway on the ground floor towards the road that runs through the village, and as we looked up, my night sight lost focus. I got the direction back, and I saw an older man (40+) with long scruffy hair and a checkered farmer style shirt leaning out the window staring at us.

I immediately tapped my buddy in dead silence, who looked up and confirmed he saw it too by squeezing my arm. Because we had LLM fitted, we used IR torches to go through the building, him staying at the door and me systematically clearing the rooms. As I started up the stairs, we heard footsteps walking towards the stairs, so we made ourselves known and stacked up together in the stairs to move up and find out who was fucking with us. We got to the top of the stairs seconds after hearing the footsteps.

No chance they could have got out, we switched to white lights and confirmed the house was clear and empty, we shrugged it off and changed overwatch. We never spoke about it to anyone. Over breakfast the following day, we overheard a few guys talking about the same guy. We never went over to confirm stories but quite interesting to know we weren't the only ones to see something in the village.

Dad In The Training Area

Roughly 0330 in Gibraltar Barracks Training Area. I'm on sentry duty from a FOB we had built earlier that day. We had been sleep-deprived for a few days, and I'm doing anything and everything to keep myself awake. About 150 meters away, I see some movement in the tree line, so I look down my SUSAT to try and get a better look.

It's a full moon, and the ambient light is quite good. I see a stereotypical dad with the white shirt, jeans, and those new balance trainers walking with speed and purpose directly towards the FOB from the tree line. As its 0300 I'm questioning whether or not this is real or my mind is playing tricks. As I'm questioning my sanity, he breaks into a full sprint directly towards the FOB entrance, and I shake the guy on sentry with me to alert him of this absolute maniac running towards us.

I go to challenge him, and before I even utter a word, he comes to a dead stop, turns 180°, and sprints back to the tree line. I'm in shock and I radio it in....my section commander comes on the net and says words to the effect of "you're a fucking idiot. There's nobody out here."

The following day another guy approaches me during my morning routine and asks about it. I tell him what happened, he said the same thing happened to him at 0400, and he was convinced he was hallucinating. We never found out who/what or why, but needless to say, we all slept with one eye open the next night.

It's not unheard of for civilians to come to the training area, but this is the height of winter. It's 0300, and the dude is not wearing any warm clothing or anything. I've wondered whether he was some late-night fitness fanatic doing interval sprints, but he wasn't dressed the part. It's something I've questioned over and over again. I don't believe in ghosts or spirits or any of that stuff, so the only logical explanation I can come up with is that the dude was mentally unwell or I was hallucinating... but then other dudes saw the same thing as me too.

Brecon

I was in an infantry regiment in the British Army. We have a training area over a large portion of Wales known as Brecon. Brecon is just grassland with a spattering of artificial square woodblocks for training areas and such. Down in the valleys, it is lovely rolling green hills with sheep everywhere, but the training area sits higher up and is exposed, windy, and nearly always raining sideways. There are about 10 to 15 old farms in the training area. They usually are a cluster of small buildings, the farmhouse, shepherd's hut, and a barn. All of them are old, made of local stone, and were probably built 200 to 300 years ago. Since being taken over by the MOD, they have been ripped out and boarded shut to be used by as staging areas or as part of the exercise itself.

In 2013 I was unfortunate enough to be given a tasking to backfill a section of NCOs on a pre leadership school course. Essentially our battalion gets them all together to put them through the mill to make sure they are best prepared to go and do the extended period with all the other regiments. It was pretty miserable, and unlike other field exercises, there was no motivation for me to be there as I was only there to make up section numbers while they rotated through command appointments.

It's late spring, so the weather was not too cold. The rest of the guys were taken to do a lesson on giving orders, so I wasn't needed. I went into one of the farm buildings to hang out. After a short while, I had this weird feeling like I was being watched.

There was no window in this room, and the doorway back into the hall only let in a bit of light. There was a hatch in the ceiling going into the attic space. No sooner had I cast my eyes onto the hatch that I noticed it was open about three inches with the opening towards me. It almost immediately slammed down when I looked at it with some force and a loud bang.

I remember feeling relatively calm like somebody is winding me up here. So, I got up and walked quickly outside to find out who was missing from the small group left at the farm, and determine who was pissing about in the loft. Everyone was chilling outside, and there was not enough time for one of them to get out of the attic unseen before I got to them.

No idea what this all was, but when I got back to the room to get my kit, I got serious goosebumps, and ran outside quick like. I have no explanation for it. The door closed with far too much force to have been just a mouse or rat running about up there. There was no wind that day and the only people within half a mile were all sat outside.

North Yorkshire

We were based on an RAF airfield in North Yorkshire that saw use by the bomber command during WW2. The place gets foggy between October and February and is generally quite eerie after 1800hrs - where the mist creeps in off the fields (like every ghost movie).

There are multiple accounts of guys and girls seeing/hearing things there. During my first month on camp, I was an orderly NCO and had to lock up the respective hanger for my subunit at 1850hrs. I was on my way back to report to the orderly Sgt at the guard room - when I saw a woman walking from RHQ and down the main road out of camp.

It was mid-October. She looks like she's on her way to a Halloween party. But to be honest, who the heck has a wimple and pinafore? She was dressed like an old-time nurse! I got to the guard room and asked everyone who the chick was. Everyone laughed and asked had I seen the ghost from the old hospital? It turns out RHQ used to be the hospital and morgue!

A month later, in the middle of the night, I was jolted awake, and I swear for the blink of an eye: I could see the silhouette of a guy wearing a WW2 sidcot suit, a really distinctive flying suit that only bomber crews wore.

Tapa Camp

British Army, about February-March time, in Tapa Camp Estonia. The weather was cold as hell but most if not all of the snow was gone.

I walked from the guardroom in one of the main accommodation blocks as guard commander that night to the smoking area behind the camp shop. All was fine. I had my cigarette alone in the shelter and started to walk back. On my walk back to the guardroom, I was walking down the main road of camp, a short walk maybe only 50-75 meters.

Walking towards me on the opposite side of the road was a hooded man in winter jacket and walking trousers, not unusual at all, as that is more or less the standard dress for British Soldiers after work hours.

But that's when it started to get weird. As he came towards me, I began to get this crushing feeling in my chest, and I couldn't stop looking into the hood he was wearing. All I could see was darkness. Like complete black, with no features or anything.

As we came level with each other, I felt his "eyes," though I couldn't see any, staring right back at me. I had the most overwhelming sense of impending doom. Like my life was over. Pure fight or flight.

As I started to move past him, it looked like his head was still following me unnaturally past the point that someone can turn their head.

I jog-walked into the light of the Guardroom hyperventilating and decided to put an end to my late-night cigarette breaks. As far as I am aware, I was the only one ever to see "him."

The Gnomes

We were on Herrick 7 in Afghanistan as young Marines in 40 Commando Royal Marines. We were in Sangin tasked with taking ground at the forward edge of the frontlines. Marines would fight through areas, taking ground, and the Army would follow up behind building FOBs and PBs to hold the hard-won territory. This is the height of Taliban violence and IED activity. Lads were getting shot and blown up regularly. They were losing legs, arms, feet and being killed. There were instances of the Taliban hanging body parts from trees to scare troops in certain areas.

Through all of this chaos, madness, and violence, we had loyal interpreters that risked their lives by being with us. They were from the area, but if found to be doing what they were doing, their families would be beheaded. To say these guys were brave is an understatement.

On a routine patrol, we came up to a new village. As we approached the town, these same brave "terps" stopped and refused to go into the village and would not say why. After much arguing and threatening not to pay them for not completing their job, they finally said they would not enter the village because it was inhabited by evil gnomes that cursed and killed people. They said they were angry, short, dark-skinned, moved quickly, and looked like little people.

Although we didn't see any gnomes in this village, those interpreters would not enter the village. Some quit on the spot over this village. These interpreters never backed down from a fight with the Taliban and routinely went through the shit with us. After all they had seen and been through... It makes me wonder how real and how evil those gnomes could have been?

Longmoor Camp

This story takes place five or six years ago at a military training ground in Britain called Longmoor Camp. Its 160 odd years old, and it has mainly fallen out of use. From what I know, it is only used by MPs and cadets. I was taking part in five-day fieldcraft (FTX for Americans), and I at some point got left alone in an OP at night watching a road that went through the middle of the woods with a single lamppost.

Full disclosure, we were military cadets. We were not issued the best equipment, so we had these old starlight scopes. Very early generation night vision optics. During the two hours, I was alone at the OP, I accidentally looked towards the streetlight with the scope and stopped myself just before I got to it. I realized at the corner of the optic picture was movement. I edged it a little more towards the light and saw pitch-black shadows moving around the light.

I looked at the light without the scope with my naked eye, and no one was there. I looked back with the scope they were there. The shadows were full-blown human-sized. The light was probably around 50m from my OP. I couldn't see them with the naked eye, only under the night vision optic. Terrified me for the rest of the time I sat stuck there.

COLOMBIAN ARMY

Almas En Pena

I was a conscript from 2014 to 2016. I was assigned to a unit in the Cauca region of Colombia. Besides being a heavy combat zone because of the FARC, ELN, narco cartels, and organized crime, the region has the most indigenous groups in Colombia.

So back in those days, we were going on patrol around an area called Totoro, very mountainous with dense forests and a lot of water. Hence, there are a few resguardos around there, which are reserved areas for those indigenous tribes. We walked all day in the wrong direction because our lieutenant didn't know how to read a map.

We had to turn around and go back, but it got dark, and the lieutenant said we had to camp there for the night. It was within one of these resguardos, but there was no one living around that little area. We saw a little clearing near a creek and decided that it was the best spot to set up camp. I should mention that the clearing was on the side of a hill, the crest was towards the west, the creek was towards the east running about 100 meters down from the clearing, and to the north and south, it was just a hillside with dense forest. The clearing seemed to be carved out in the hill, so it was flat.

I remember a corporal saying how weird it was that such a place was that quiet. Usually, the jungle is loud with wildlife and all that. Still, we didn't pay attention to it as we thought it was maybe due to all the hunting and human intervention in that area, so we just went to sleep. About two hours in, one of our sentries came running to wake up the corporal and tell him that he saw someone walk around the creek.

He thought that it was a native, but after that person went up the

225

creek, it disappeared and also made no sound. He was dismissed and an hour went by with another sentry reporting he saw someone just standing on top of a tree branch. The sentry freaked out and flashed a light on the figure, but didn't see him anymore. So he came running to the corporal again, told him what he had seen, and that he didn't want to go to his post alone again. So, they put us in groups of two and told us to stand to watch all night. I went with the guy that was standing post near the creek

We didn't see anything for like two hours, but around midnight, the guy I was with saw a dude standing on a big rock that was in the middle of the creek. He told me, and I saw it. I told him to get the corporal as I sat there and watched it. He came back with the corporal; the corporal saw it as we both did and he decided to flash a light on this figure. But as soon as he did, the figure disappeared, and the rock was empty.

The corporal went up, told our lieutenant who was sleeping. The lieutenant said that a patrol should be sent there to see what it was and went back to sleep. Corporal came back down to us and said, "there's no way in hell I'm sending anyone down there," so he just decided to stay with us watching what was up. Then a call came on the radio that we weren't supposed to be using because it was too loud, and it was another sentry pair that was towards the west side of the hill we were camping on. This sentry pair overlooked the whole campsite.

The guys on top called in on the radio, corporal got mad as fuck but they just basically talked over him. They were saying that they were watching "people" walk around right in front of us. They were shocked that we weren't doing anything. Honestly, we didn't see any movement.

We were staring at the creek, but after they told us that, we just started scanning the whole area. We didn't see anything but heard a splash in the stream. It could've been anything, just a coincidence, but by that point, the corporal said fuck it. Told everyone to come back to the campsite, woke the lieutenant up, and the few other guys that were sleeping at the campsite. We were leaving.

We packed our stuff and started walking. It was about 0400 at that point, we walked until we found a little community of houses. The lieutenant talked to someone there, and they let us camp near them. It was about 0600 when that happened, so most of us were tired as fuck. They let us sleep, after we woke up, we talked to some of the people in that community. They told us that the little clearing was an ancient burial site, that no one was allowed to go there, mainly not the kids. Because according to them: "el rio de los come," which roughly means "the river eats them."

They believe that there is a spirit who roams the creek. If someone is walking around there alone, it lures them into the stream, drowns them, and vanishes. They say that some of the other spirits are angry and dangerous because they're the spirits of the natives that were massacred during the Spanish campaigns that aimed to colonize all that area. Hence, they are "Almas en Pena."

I don't know how to translate, but it's something like "grieving souls," they told us to stay the fuck away from that place. They did a little ritual to "cleanse" us with smoke. They then warned us to stay away from the creek and never, ever walk on places that seem oddly clean, with short grass and some weirdly placed rocks on them. Most likely they're just mass graveyards of native people.

IRISH ARMY

The Airfield

I was stationed at a small airfield camp that we took back from the British in 1920. One night, a few of us stayed in the accommodation after a night on the sauce. Our room was packed and had a three-seater couch in the center facing the TV.

I got woken up at 0530 by something and looked over at one of the lads on the couch to see a figure behind the sofa that resembled my other mate. The dark figure was the same height, shape and even had the distinct hair outline as my mate. I called out to thinking it was him messing with the lad on the couch.

I called out to the figure three times, and then I saw my actual mate moving in his bed. As I looked back, I saw the figure slowly slide down behind the back of the couch, and I rolled the fuck over in bed.

No idea what it was, but it was like the perfect shadow outline of my mate. He has a sharp hairline, and when he turns, you can tell it's his head; The figure had the exact sharp hair line. Whatever it was, was creepy as fuck

RUSSIAN ARMED FORCES

"No borders hold us"

I have a story from my uncle who was in the Red Army. He was from Uzbekistan, but was conscripted and stationed in Siberia back when it was under the USSR. My uncle was tasked to work at a radar station. Basically, this turned out to be the most desolate and boring assignment possible. Nothing ever happened there, and there was literally nothing in the sky.

One day late into the winter, he suddenly starts getting contacts on his radar. He's startled as he's never seen anything out there before. He starts getting more and more contacts on screen and begins to think to himself, "holy fuck it's happening." Dozens and dozens more blips begin to appear and everyone in his station begins to fear this is the beginning of the end.

He tries to make contact on the open mic radio, and demands identification. At first there's nothing. Then a scratchy response… it's a voice, but it's too distorted to be anything human.

"We are the unseen. We go where we wish, no borders hold us."

Then silence. All the blips vanish from the screen all at once. It was as if they were never there to begin with.

My uncle believes they were Jinn (from his Islamic faith). What he heard the voice say matches what the Islamic world knows of the Jinn. Or so he believes.

[The following stories were provided by a US Army Soldier, who immigrated from Russia and became a naturalized US citizen. This Soldier was conscripted into the Russian Armed Forces prior to their time in the US Army. This Soldier provides two experiences from their time in the VDV, the Russian Paratroopers.]

The VDV Part I - Whispers In The Woods

Before I became a US citizen and joined the US Army, I was in the VDV (Russian Paratroopers) from 2008-2013. During my time, I did two combat rotations, one being in Chechnya, the other being in Dagestan. During my first rotation in Chechnya, it was the early spring of 2009. The rain was non-stop, and the fog was thick like porridge. Days out there shifted between cold and hellishly hot.

I was conducting a patrol in the dead of night with my sentry team, a group of four men: Vasya, Kirill, Alyosha, and myself. It had been raining the whole day, and it didn't seem like it was going to stop for the night either. The woods were thick and impenetrable, and any noise was nonexistent besides our own footfalls. My team was walking through the woods when all of a sudden we see what looks like torches in front of us. We turned and looked at each other, obviously worried about meeting insurgents in this pitch blackness.

That's when the whispers started happening. It didn't make sense to me, it sounded like the trees were talking. Like the voices were coming from every direction at once. But I couldn't make out anything they said. But it was different for Vasya.

Vasya began to call out "Papa? What do you mean you want me close to you?" He starts taking off into the forest and I mean dead sprinting towards those lights that appeared. He dropped his rifle and stripped off all his gear and proceeded to run through brambles and bushes like they didn't matter. The other three of us were barely keeping up with him as he continues to yell for his father, asking if he is cold and hungry.

We finally caught up to him. He just stopped at this small clearing in the forest, at the edge of a peatbog. He falls to his knees and says to us, "I'd like to go home now." We drag him back to camp and explain to our NCO in charge why we were thirty minutes late. We laid in our bedrolls looking at each other in shock, trying not to cry. The villagers in many different places in Russia talk about fairy lights or cappers, which will lead people into the swamps to their deaths.

The VDV Part II - Mongolian Death Worm

Another training exercise I was one was with the Mongolian and Kazakhstani Army. I was pretty much walking around a desert for a month and wondering when I would die of heatstroke. There was a point where our groups were walking around these pumice/sandstone hills. If you don't know, pumice is a very porous stone with natural holes showing through, and after enough time these holes get big enough to fit a small man or a large dog.

I was on night watch on behind a KORD machine gun. We had these giant IR/thermals attached to them. I was scanning the terrain (and more or less sleeping) when I see what appears to be a thermal image resembling one of those inflatable tube men (the kind you see at used car dealerships in the US). It's about 100m out, on the slope of a hill. I blink and close my eyes. When I open them I still see this thing moving from side to side, just like one of those inflatable tube men but with no arms.

I turned on the floodlight attached to the KORD, and saw for a split second this massive fucking caterpillar. It was about the size of a horse! Its poking out of one of those large holes in the pumice and it slinks back down after I shine a light on it.

I remember in vivid detail what this thing looked like: it was the same amber color as a cockroach and I counted eight limbs from what I saw. I can only guess it was maybe quarter of the full length of this thing sticking out of the hole. Its "face" looked exactly like a wood grub.

I shouted in legitimate surprise and hear something behind me. I turn around and a Kazak Soldier had been watching me. He promptly explained I had seen a "Mongolian Death Worm." To be honest, I have no explanation for what I could have seen otherwise.

231

THIS COMPLETES TALES FROM THE GRID SQUARE

VOLUME I

*****

Stay tuned for Volume II of Tales From The Grid Square!

Authors Final Note

I would like to extend a sincere "Thank You" to every person who helped make this book a reality. To my wonderful family: thank you for supporting me and motivating me. To all the Service Members, Veterans, and their Families that have submitted stories on their behalf; thank you for sharing your experiences with me. Thank you for your service.

Again, a reminder to the reader: it is 100% impossible for me to verify any of these stories, so take these stories with a "grain of salt." **These stories are not intended to provide one hundred percent irrefutable proof of the paranormal.** I did not write this book to convince you to believe or not to believe. Rather I share these stories with you to give a voice to Veterans and Service Members who have had experiences that defy normality.

"Nick Orton" is a pseudonym. The author of this book is the founder of Tales From The Grid Square and is still a current active-duty member of the US Military. For the sake of anonymity, the author has omitted their true name while they remain in the service.

However, if you are a currently serving member of the military (United States or otherwise), a veteran, a military family member, a nurse, police officer or firefighter and have an experience of your own (or know someone who does) please reach out to speak to the Founder of Tales From The Grid Square via:

Instagram: @Tales_From_The_Gridsquare (Primary Account)

                      @TFTG_Redux (Alternate Account)

Email: TalesFromTheGridsquare@gmail.com

The world is a strange place, with many mysteries left unsolved. I leave it to you to search for answers and come up with your own conclusions. To quote a friend who has helped me along the way:

"The truth will set you free, but first it will piss you off."

Glossary Of Terms

(Because the military loves acronyms)

A-10   *The premier tank busting attack CAS platform (BRRRRR)*

ABU   *Airman Battle Uniform*

AC130   *The gunship version of the C-130 cargo plane*

ACU   *Army Combat Uniform (also the used to refer to the horrible gravel color digital uniforms of the GWOT)*

AF   *Air Force*

AFT   *Behind the ship*

AFV   *Armored Fighting Vehicle*

AFB   *Air Force Base*

AIT   *Advanced Initial Training*

AFRL   *Air Force Research Laboratory*

AK   *Slang for the AK-47 rifle and its successors*

ANON   *Anonymous*

ANSF   *Afghanistan Security Force*

A-School   *Accession training where sailors go to receive technical training in their MOS.*

AOD   *Administrative Officer of the Day*

B2   *The wedge-shaped stealth bomber, commonly mistaken for a UFO*

B52   *Cold War era heavy bomber still in use today*

BCT   *Basic Combat Training*

BCT   *Brigade Combat Team*

BDE   *Brigade*

BMAT   *Ballistic Missile Analyst Technician*

BMQ   *Canadian basic training program for future NCOs*

BLUFOR   *Blue Force (aka the good guys)*

BN   *Battalion*

BOW   *The front of the ship*

BTW   *By the Way*

C6   *General Purpose Machine Gun used by the CAF*

CAC   *Common Access Card*

CAB   *Combat Aviation BDE*

CALFEX	*Combined Arms Live Fire Exercise*
CAP	*Civil Air Patrol*
CBRN	*Chemical, Biological, Radiological and Nuclear*
CDTC	*Canadian Division Training Center*
CFB	*Canadian Forces Base*
CIVMAR	*Civilian Mariner (The modern merchant marine)*
CLU	*A containerized shelter used during the GWOT*
CO	*Commanding Officer*
COB	*Contingency Operating Base*
COC	*Chain of Command*
COP	*Combat Outpost*
CP	*Command Post*
CROW	*Common Remotely Operated Weapon Station*
CST	*Cadet Summer Training*
CQ	*Charge of Quarters (the duty watches in the barracks)*
CVW	*Carrier Air Wing*
CWO	*Chief Warrant Officer (might as well be a cryptid themselves)*
DCU	*Desert Combat Uniform (of Gulf War and early GWOT fame)*
DDG	*Guided Missile Destroyer*
DFAC	*Dining Facility (where taste goes to die)*
DI	*Drill Instructor*
DLI	*Defense Language Institute*
DNCO	*Duty Non-Commissioned Officer*
DP-1	Canadian Army Battle School
DS	*Drill Sergeant*
DTA	*Donnelly Training Area (Alaska)*
DZ	*Drop Zone*
ECP	*Entry Control Point*
EFMB	*Expert Field Medic Badge*
ELN	*National Liberation Army (Colombian left-wing revolutionary group)*
EOD	*Explosive Ordnance Disposal*
F-14	*Former premier interceptor of the US Navy (and Top Gun fame)*
F-22	*Current USAF "stealth fighter"*

F-117 *The Knighthawk, the original stealth bomber of the Cold War*

FASCAM *Family of scatter able mines*

FAP *Family Advocacy Program*

FARC *Revolutionary Armed Forces of Colombia – Peoples Liberation Army*

FC-A *Field Calibration Activates*

Firebase *Fire Support Base*

FLIR *Forward-Looking Infrared Camera*

FMF *Fleet Marine Force*

GBOSS *Ground Based Operational Surveillance System*

GBH *Grievous Bodily Harm*

GI *General Issue*

GITA *Ground Instructional Training Aircraft*

GITMO *Guantanamo Bay, Cuba*

G-MAN *Aka "Geronimo" the infamous OPFOR units of the Army (our worst enemy is literally ourselves)*

GM *Gunners Mate*

GMG *Grenade Machine Gun*

GPS *Global Positioning System*

GTFO *Get the FUCK out*

GySgt *Gunnery Sergeant*

HBCT *Heavy Brigade Combat Team*

HF *High Frequency*

HLZ *Helicopter Landing Zone*

HM *Hospital Corpsmen*

HMMWV *Humvee (probably deadlined in a motor pool near you)*

HOG *Hunter Of Gunmen, USMC sniper term (that just sounds badass)*

HQ *Headquarters*

IAR *Infantry Automatic Rifle*

IC *Incident Command*

ID *Identification*

IED *Improvised Explosive Device*

IFF *Identify Friend or Foe*

IHG *Hotel chain that now runs all Army lodging*

ITB *Infantry Training Battalion*

IR	*Infrared*
IVO	*In Vicinity Of*
JBLM	*Joint Base Lewis-McChord*
JRTC	*Joint Readiness Training Center (where light infantry units go to suffer in Louisiana)*
JMRC	*Joint Mission Readiness Center (where all Europe centric US Army units go to suffer in Germany)*
K9	*Dogs (or military puppers if you will)*
KAF	*Kandahar Airfield*
KORD	*Russian 12.7mm heavy machine gun*
LAR	*Light Armored Reconnaissance Battalion*
Land Nav	*Land Navigation (the bane of every 2LT)*
LCpl	*Lance Corporal (The E4 mafia of the USMC)*
LDA	*Linear Danger Area*
LGOP	*Little Groups Of Paratroopers*
LLDR	*Lightweight Laser Designator Rangefinder*
LLM	*Launcher Loader Module*
LMTV	*Light Medium Tactical Vehicle*
LP	*Listening Post*
LRS	*Long-Range Surveillance*
LT	*Lieutenant (the bane of all enlisted)*
M2	*The indomitable .50cal machine gun ('Ma Deuce if you will)*
M17/M9	*Standard issue 9mm Army side arm*
M4/M16	*The standard issue 5.56mm weapon of the US Military*
M60	*Vietnam era 7.62MM machine gun (AKA THE PIG)*
M240	*The modern day 7.62MM machine gun of the US Military*
M249	*The 5.56MM machine gun of the US Military (aka the SAW)*
M988	*Derivative of the Humvee*
MAJ	*Major, O-4 rank (who needs to leave the office and go spend time with their family)*
MBT	*Main Battle Tank*
MCAS	*Marine Corps Air Station*
MCLC	*Mine Clearing Line Charge*
MCRD	*Marine Corps Recruit Depot*
MEV	*Medical Evacuation Vehicle*

MILES Multiple Integrated Laser Engagement System (basically laser tag for the military)

MIB Men In black

MM Motor Machinist

MOD Ministry Of Defense

MO Modus Operandi

MOUT Military Operations In Urban Terrain

MP Military Police

MP Motor Pool

MPRC Manpower and Personnel Readiness Center

MRE Meals Ready to Eat (the Pizza one is the best, deal with it)

MSR Main Supply Route

MWR Military Welfare and Recreation (a source for fun activities)

MQ-9 Aka The Reaper, the unmanned (and armed) eye in the sky

NASA National Aeronautics and Space Administration

NAF Naval Air Facility

NAS Naval Air Station

NATO North Atlantic Treaty Organization

NCO Non-Commissioned Officer (the backbone of the US Armed Forces)

NCOIC Non-Commissioned Officer In Charge

NETOPS Network Operations

NSTR Nothing Significant To Support

NTC National Training Center (where the armored brigades of the Army go to suffer in the heat)

NTSB National Transportation Safety Board

NVA North Vietnamese Army

NVG Night Vision Goggles

OCP Occupational Camouflage Pattern

OCS Officer Candidate School

OEF Operation Enduring Freedom

OIC Officer/Overall In Charge

OIF Operation Iraqi Freedom

OC Officer Candidate

OC/T (OC) Observer Coach/Trainer (tormentor of the RTU)

OG Original

Oki	*Abbreviation for Okinawa*
OOD	*Officer Of the Day*
OP	*Observation Post*
OPFOR	*Opposing Force (the pretend bad guys)*
OSUT	*Infantry One Station Training*
OSV	*Opposing Force Surrogate Vehicle*
PB	*Patrol Base*
PE	*Program Element*
PEQ15	*The AN/PEQ-15, also known as the Advanced Target Pointer Illuminator Aiming Light (ATPIAL)*
PFC	*Private First Class (E-3 of the Army enlisted ranks)*
PIG	*Professionally Instructed Gunmen, USMC sniper language*
PLT	*Platoon*
PMO	*Provost Marshal (aka the MPs)*
POOD	*Petty Officer Of the Deck*
PSG	*Platoon Sergeant (Platoon Daddy if you will)*
PSQ20	*The AN/PSQ-20 Enhanced Night Vision Goggle (ENVG) is a third-generation passive monocular night vision device*
PT	*Physical Training; PT is free*
PTA	*Pōhakuloa Training Area*
PWAY	*Passageway*
PVT	*Private, E-1 of enlisted ranks in the Army and Marines*
PX	*Post Exchange*
QRF	*Quick Reaction Force*
RAF	*Royal Airforce*
Raven	*A small, hand launched surveillance drone (basically a remote-control plane)*
RIMPAC	*The yearly "Rim of the Pacific" naval exercise involving the US Navy and others*
RO	*Ranking Officer*
ROM	*Restriction Of Movement*
RN	*Registered Nurse*
RTO	*Radio Telephone Operator*
RTU	*Rotational Unit*
RUBA	*Rotational Unit Base Area*
SATCOM	*Satellite Communications*

SAW Squad Automatic Weapon (aka the M249)

SBCT Stryker Brigade Combat Team

SDO Staff Duty Officer

SF Special Forces (the cool dudes with the fancy gear)

SGT Sergeant

SH1 Ships Serviceman First Class

SKT Small Kill Team

SNCO Senior Non-Commissioned Officer

SNOOPIE Photographic Interpretation and Examination

SOG Sergeant of the Guard

SSgt (SSG) Staff Sergeant (E-6 enlisted rank)

Stryker The Army's eight wheeled infantry fighting vehicle

STX Situational Training Exercise

SUSAT Sight Unit Small Arms Trilux (British Army combat optic)

SWO Surface Warfare Officer

SWO Staff Weather Officer

TA50 Army designation for basic issued gear

TA Training Area

TAD Temporary Additional Duty

TC Truck Commander

TCP Traffic Control Point

TDY Temporary Duty Yet Assigned

Tech V (Technical) Makeshift tactical vehicle (for example see the famous Toyota Hilux)

TF Task Force (also the abbreviation for "Tha Fuck?!")

TIC Troops In Contact

TL Team Leader

TOC Tactical Operations Center

UAP Unidentified Airborne Object (because UFO wasn't good enough)

UDP Unit Deployment Program

UFO Unidentified Flying Object

USAF United States Air Force

USMA United States Military Academy, aka WestPoint (bunch of nerds)

USMC United States Marine Corps (a literal cult)

USO	*Unidentified Submerged Object*
USO	*United Service Organization (visit your local one)*
USSR	*Union of Soviet Republics*
UXO	*Unexploded Ordnance*
X-33	*Former Supersonic X-Plane*
XO	*Executive Officer*
VBIED	*Vehicle Borne IED*
VDV	*Vozdushno-Desantnye Voyska (Russian Federation Airborne Forces)*
Woobie	*The legendary, and incredibly warm military issued poncho liner. More uses than just a blanket*
0311	*Marine Corps Infantry Designator*
11B	*Army Infantry Designator*
12M	*Army Firefighter Designator*

28 September 2023
North Haven, CT
Made in United States